PRAISE FOR #FULLYCHARGED

I am totally geeking out about *#FULLYCHARGED!* This book is a must read for anyone connected to the EDU world. Three incredible voices combine to help readers understand the science of education, the art of teaching, and how a critical mix of meeting Bloom skills and Maslow needs can shift the way we support our students.

Julie Adams, PJ Caposey, and Rosa Isiah provide the research as to why we must meet Maslow's in order to cultivate Bloom's, and the powerful tools to help us do it. They also throw down a challenge that we should all work toward…to have our schools compete with Disneyland for the title "The Happiest Place on Earth."

This book serves as a guide to help shift the approach we take as we work to empower students, parents, and staff, and design school culture where all members thrive!

> Ann Kozma
> Teacher on Special Assignment, California
> @annkozma723

*   *   *   *   *

We live in a world where students experience adversities that were not around when I was in school. Yet, we continue to expect students who face high levels of stress to perform at a high level of achievement. Why? Because other students are making it happen. Comparison is a danger we face, since adversities are a perception based on the person who is involved and how they view the adversity.

Knowing this, I personally do not feel there is a more important time than now to take a deeper dive into the needs of human capacity, pertaining to mental, social, physical, and emotional needs, particularly with our students.

What makes me want to stand up and shout "Woo hoo!" is that *#FULLYCHARGED* addresses these core issues head on, but through the lens of brain research and Maslow's Hierarchy of Needs.

What makes a student unmotivated?

How can the brain thrive in an ecosystem that often drains the brain?

Why are relationships an integral part in student learning?

These are the powerful and important questions we should be pondering and the authors tackle them all. This book is a resource to help facilitate such thinking, while providing provocative insight into what is happening below the layers of our students. Unveil the layers and implement the insights provided to become *#FULLYCHARGED!*

> LaVonna Roth
> Lead Illuminator, Creator, and Founder of Ignite Your
> S.H.I.N.E., Florida
> @LaVonnaRoth

*   *   *   *   *

#FULLYCHARGED is a remarkably thoughtful, provocative, and useful tool for educators. This book is alive with new insights, concepts, and thoughtful strategies that can be utilized by any reader to build a deeper understanding of the impact that chronic stress plays in the role of social and academic growth.

Within the last several decades, environmental stress has increased to unprecedented levels. The authors share the importance of dealing with our students' social-emotional well-being, so they develop the positive state of mind for learning. Addressing social-emotional needs according to "Maslow's Hierarchy" is necessary for the body and mind to effectively achieve higher levels of performance or the advancement of "Blooms." Therefore, "Maslow before Bloom" becomes the context for growth.

The authors successfully detail the negative impact that stress, and more importantly, chronic stress, plays in human development. When parents, teachers, and leaders more effectively understand this impact, they are more capable of addressing the social and academic needs of their students. The book is filled with powerful strategies to address the adverse effects of stress and is a must read for parents, teachers, and leaders.

Art Fessler
Superintendent of Schools, CCSD 59, Illinois
@afess7

* * * * *

#FULLYCHARGED provides a clear roadmap to empowering the ideal leadership trifecta necessary to create a powerful school experience for our students, parents, and staff!

Marlena Gross-Taylor
Author, Speaker, Founder of @EduGladiators, Tennessee
@mgrosstaylor

* * * * *

Every educator needs to read this book! It is loaded with practical and brain-friendly strategies that we can utilize to reach EVERY student, parent, and staff member. Julie, PJ, and Rosa illustrate the essence of what education is all about—reaching, supporting, engaging, and teaching every student, every day.

While reading, I was literally brought to tears, thought "WOW," nodded my head in agreement, and went "Hmmm…" as I dug deeper into this thought-provoking resource for educators. I daresay that the authors will educate you in areas that you may not have thought about. They will inspire you with strategies that you will want to implement immediately.

These three authors—the superintendent, the principal, and the teacher/coach—have "touched all the bases" for each educator, no matter what role you serve. They provide the latest research-backed strategies that will work to ignite your students' learning and catapult their achievement.

Through testimonies and research, the authors explain the importance of creating positive relationships and the connection to learning. They illustrate how they each worked to know, care for, empathize with, and support individual students in different ways depending on their needs. #FULLYCHARGED supports and proves the statement, "You must meet Maslow, before you address Bloom."

I have been fortunate to have each of the authors in my PLN on Twitter and have benefitted from their knowledge and gifts. I pray that these words inspire you to be a leader and educator of significance, as they have inspired me.

Hal Roberts
Retired Superintendent, Keynote Speaker, Author,
Consultant, Texas
@HalLRoberts

*   *   *   *   *

I have been in education for nearly 20 years and over that time there has been one constant: *improve instruction*. Effective instruction is vital, yet we as educators are missing the bigger picture when that is our singular goal. *#FULLYCHARGED* is a holistic approach to improving learning outcomes, by addressing both the Maslow and Bloom needs for all of us in the educational system: our students, parents, and staff. The authors identify the areas where we must start to make a positive change in order to increase success. It's not just about focusing on pedagogy, but first on every person's Maslow needs. As we assess Maslow's, we can then apply the knowledge and strategies to strengthen students, staff, and parents. *#FULLYCHARGED* also gives us more applicable knowledge in Bloom's Taxonomy than any other book I have read, by providing a thorough toolkit of strategies.

#FULLYCHARGED is the first and only holistic approach that focuses on meeting all the capacity needs of the people involved in education. I have personally worked with Julie Adams and read the books of PJ Caposey, and have utilized their practices in my own district and witnessed great improvement. I'm thankful that they, along with Rosa Isiah, have provided all of their research and strategies in one powerful resource.

I urge educators at all levels to dive deep into this book, to learn how we can best improve the lives of our students, parents, and staff, in order to create the positive educational experience our students deserve.

John Hannah
Superintendent, Morton School District, Washington

*   *   *   *   *

#FULLYCHARGED is a must read for educators who truly want to address the challenges facing urban education. Julie Adams, PJ Caposey, and Rosa Isiah provide accessible research to support their recommendations that will assist all school leaders in creating environments that are inclusive of all stakeholders.

I appreciate that this book addresses parent needs, which are vital, though sometimes a missing component when making decisions. *#FULLYCHARGED* creates the space for schools to really delve into how their environment is structured and identifies the barriers to be addressed to increase access for all stakeholders in the school community. It provides educators with resources that will improve the experiences and success of our students, parents, and staff.

Yetunde Reeves
Nationally Board Certified Teacher, Administrator,
Consultant, Washington D.C.

*   *   *   *   *

#FULLYCHARGED talks about what needs to be talked about! Being present, going the extra mile for a child, waking up ready to attack the day, and the authors do so with validated research, strategies, and their own personal stories from education weaved in. You'll keep reading because you'll be continuously learning and wanting more from each page, and then you will have the tools to make positive changes in your classroom, school, or district.

Adam Welcome
Author, Director of Innovation, Speaker, California
@awelcome

*　　*　　*　　*　　*

Any teacher knows that what we do in the classroom is a delicate balance. We need to know pedagogy, research, and data to implement best practices. But we also need to understand our students and the school climate so we can effectively monitor and adjust on a regular basis. This book is a beautiful blend of the art and science of teaching. It provides helpful strategies to improve our art, and they are all backed up with scientific research to strengthen our students, parents, and staff.

Shannon Hugo
Middle School Teacher, South Carolina

*　　*　　*　　*　　*

Teachers and administrators can overemphasize test scores, student growth, and this week's learning targets. However, our students sometimes enter the schoolhouse doors broken, hungry, tired, abused, and neglected. #FULLYCHARGED is a thought-provoking book that outlines strategies for supporting the whole child. The authors provide a powerful plan to help your staff and parents have a greater impact and positively transform lives.

Steven Weber
Associate Superintendent for Teaching & Learning,
Fayetteville Public Schools, Arkansas

*　　*　　*　　*　　*

Combining powerful neuroscience and years of real-world educational experience, Julie Adams, PJ Caposey, and Rosa Isiah have crafted a masterful message that blends the work of Maslow and Bloom in a way that finally makes sense. The academic and social-emotional needs of students cannot, and should not, be separated. #FULLYCHARGED is a call-to-arms for educators everywhere who understand that teaching the whole child is, ultimately, the only successful path.

Dave Burgess
New York Times Best-Selling Author of *Teach Like a Pirate*
President of Dave Burgess Consulting, Inc., California
@burgessdave

#FULLYCHARGED

140 Battery Charging
Maslow & Bloom Strategies
for
Students, Parents, and Staff

Julie Adams
PJ Caposey
Rosa Isiah

ISBN: 978-1-60679-432-6
Library of Congress Control Number: 2018942675
Book layout: Cheery Sugabo
Cover design: Cheery Sugabo
Front cover photo: Enmaler/Shutterstock.com

Healthy Learning
P.O. Box 1828
Monterey, CA 93942
www.healthylearning.com

Acknowledgments

First, thank you Rosa and PJ for your expertise, humor, and commitment to coauthoring this book and for sharing your thoughtful narratives and strategies in order to strengthen and encourage others. I have truly enjoyed this collaboration with you both!

To my amazing husband, Chris, and our daughters, Madeline and Grace, thank you for your smiles, hugs, love, and support, especially when I take on a project like this. You all demonstrate #FULLYCHARGED hearts to serve others, and I couldn't do it without you.

Thank you to my students, families, and colleagues for the opportunity to learn and grow with you all.

Thank you Rebecca LeRoux of B43 Productions for recording our vlogs, Shannon Hugo for manuscript editing, and Mike Colon for photo editing.

Thank you God, for providing me the opportunity to serve You and others.

—Julie Adams

*   *   *   *   *

I want to thank the dynamic duo of Rosa and Julie. I believe in this book and the impact it can have. Thank you both for all you have done for me as a professional, but even more importantly as a thinker. Writing this book collaboratively helped to shift many of my paradigms. Thank you.

Thank you to my family: Jacquie, Jameson, Jackson, Caroline, and Anthony. The time it takes for me to pursue my dream of making a dent in the educational realm, takes time away from you. Thank you for your support and understanding.

Lastly, thank you to the incredible Staff, Leadership Team, and Board of Education of Meridian CUSD 223. Your support and belief in me means more than you know.

—PJ Caposey

*   *   *   *   *

Dreams become reality with passion, determination, and the encouragement of those we love. My husband, Mike, and my beautiful children, Malcolm and Ruby, are my encouragers. They are my *why*. I am thankful for their unconditional love and unwavering support. I love them dearly for helping me make my dreams come true...and for a million other reasons.

Thank you, Julie Adams, for inviting me to be part of this great project. It's an unbelievable honor to work with you and PJ Caposey. I've learned a great deal from both of you and look forward to our #FULLYCHARGED journey.

—Rosa Isiah

Contents

SECTION 2: GOT SKILLS?

*   *   *   *   *

Please visit
effectiveteachingpd.com
or
mbsimplesolution.com
to view the Author Chats for each chapter
and
take our 21 Day Challenge to charge up your battery!

Introduction

"What's the point, Mrs. Adams?"

Brian was one of my eighth grade students who routinely asked this question.

He was transferred into my class after being kicked out of a few other classes. He came from a single-parent, high-poverty, stressful environment, and he regularly looked to pick a fight with anyone and everyone.

Academically, he struggled with literacy and numeracy; therefore, he frequently did not earn passing grades, which only compounded his frustrations.

He had unsuccessfully been in and out of our district's academic interventions for years.

He was a grenade just begging for the pin to be pulled.

And then one day...it was.

CHAPTER 1
#FULLYCHARGED

"Great leaders don't set out to be a leader...they set out to make a difference. It's never about the role, always about the goal."

—Lisa Haisha

What is your goal as an educator?

Many would say to increase Students' skills, be a positive role model, or to help establish an environment where Students can be successful.

Those are valuable goals indeed.

But what is our ULTIMATE goal?

THE ULTIMATE GOAL OF EDUCATION

There are two goals in education: the first is to help Students develop the skills to earn a living and the second is to help them develop the skills to live a life of value. Education is the foundation of a successful democratic society; an effective educational system, therefore, meets both of these goals to ultimately develop human and leadership capacity.

For our society to be prosperous, we need strong leadership in all realms: home, school, community, government, and industry. Our educational system is one of the most influential components in whether we are growing the capacity to accomplish this goal.

In the past, leadership was often about dominating brawn and forcing others into submission; it was the "my way or the highway" mentality. We now challenge that mentality as we are more educated and resourceful and, therefore, no longer submissive. As a result, a mindset shift has occurred in terms of effective leadership.

Simon Sinek, a leadership consultant, captures the essence of the old mindset versus the new, "Leadership is not about being in charge. Leadership is about taking care of those in your charge."

Twenty-first century leadership is the ability to strengthen, encourage, and take care of those in our charge; this is what determines whether we live a life of value. Our ability to care for others increases the likelihood that all members of our society have the skill, will, and support to collaboratively contribute to our success.

Some are born with this ability; some are not. That is why it's more important than ever that we, as educators, cultivate this capacity in our Students, Parents (Caregivers), and Staff.

Success is, therefore, not by chance, but by design.

Why are a Superintendent (PJ), a Principal (Rosa), and a Teacher/Cognitive Coach (Julie) writing a book about designing a leadership culture in our school systems? It's simple. Schools are a delicate ecosystem with limited resources that support a variety of consumers and producers. To maximize our efficiency and resources, we must be laser-focused in our ultimate objective: to raise competent, confident, compassionate, and creative, critical thinkers who positively impact, or add value to, society.

A leadership-focused school system strengthens society when it's designed to systematically develop what we call the 5 Cs of Leadership:

- Competence: Having the skills to complete a task successfully
- Confidence: Feeling competent and assured in one's own abilities
- Compassion: Empathizing with and sympathizing for others
- Creativity: Using efficiency, imagination, and innovation for problem-solving
- Critical thinking: Analyzing, evaluating, and problem-solving

We are passionate about and dedicated to this goal. We hope to partner with you by sharing this message and various resources, to be even more successful in cultivating capacity in our Student/Parent/Staff populations.

IS LEADERSHIP CAPACITY ROCKET SCIENCE?

Recently, I (Julie) was chatting with a rocket scientist whose daughter plays softball with my daughter. Out of curiosity, I asked him what the term "rocket science" meant to him. He intricately explained how complicated it was to design an object that efficiently races through space at a speed of at least 17,000 mph, while navigating potential dangers, in order to successfully reach the target. To be successful, one has to be skilled in both the art and science of building a rocket. If one detail is miscalculated in the design, environmental conditions, or construction, then time, energy, and precious resources are wasted, and the awesome potential, or goal, is not achieved.

This principle applies to designing effective learning environments. We are tasked with the responsibility AND opportunity to help strengthen young minds, who in essence, will race through space at lightning speed toward a finish line. Due to time, environmental factors, and resource limitations, all elements, design, and implementation must be carefully considered and maximized, so we may achieve our ultimate goal.

In other words, designing an effective environment that grows human and leadership capacity is complex and requires art and (neuro)science, just as building a rocket does.

According to Dr. Judy Willis, author of *Research-Based Strategies That Ignite Student Learning:* "Information obtained through brain imaging…during the learning process has given us a *science* of education to add to our already powerful knowledge of the *art* of teaching. Educational professionals who understand the relevant aspects of brain development, alertness, attention, and memory storage and retrieval, and who use the strategies derived from this research, will find their work becoming more effective and exciting and will find their students more engaged."

This book will serve as a manifesto in blending the art and science of developing a supportive learning culture so ALL members of our ecosystem—Students, Parents, and Staff—will thrive and meet their full potential in becoming compassionate, problem-solving leaders who are willing and able to strengthen and serve others. We are capitalizing Students, Parents, and Staff and treating them as a proper noun to serve as a visual reminder that they are more than clients or stakeholders; they are the reason we exist, a BIG deal, and they all require Maslow and Bloom specialized attention to be successful.

It can be complicated to design a culture in which leadership capacity flourishes; otherwise every school, industry, and governmental system would already be doing it. Why is it complicated? Because you're dealing with both emotional and academic intelligence, or the heart and the mind. Don't let anyone tell you that increasing Student motivation or achievement is simple…just build relationship. We'll provide and explain the neuroscience that shows why that is a vital component, but also why it's more complicated than it sounds.

Achieving it is, in fact, rocket science.

OUR RECHARGEABLE BATTERY

Contrary to popular belief, we have LIMITED cognitive capacity every day.

Every morning we wake up with a rechargeable battery, our brain. Our recent environmental conditions and choices determine how charged our battery is.

If our basic needs have been met, then we often have a fully charged battery.

If not, then we start the day with only a partial charge, which can lead to trouble, as we will not have the critical thinking and creative capacity, or battery charge, to successfully complete tasks.

Recently, researchers have focused on understanding cognitive capacity and discovered a phenomenon called "decision fatigue." Every decision we make absorbs cognitive energy and drains our battery little by little. The more stressful the decision, the more it drains capacity.

This is why Steve Jobs and Albert Einstein often wore the same clothes nearly every day. They reportedly didn't want to waste precious brainpower on small decisions, so they created routines for their clothing, food, and such.

We make tens of thousands of decisions throughout the day. It is helpful to know the environmental conditions that keep our brains #FULLYCHARGED so we can effectively serve as leaders and strengthen and care for others.

It is also vital to know how to recharge, when we are too drained to care for others. There are many powerful ways to naturally charge our battery.

Natural chargers include:
- Exercising
- Listening to positive, upbeat music
- Praying/meditating
- Laughing
- Spending time outside absorbing Vitamin D
- Consuming organic fruits, vegetables, and lean protein
- Engaging in supportive "social connectedness"
- Helping and serving others
- Playing a fun card or board game
- Sleeping
- Learning a new skill
- Feeling purposeful and working toward a goal
- Giving a sincere compliment
- Deep breathing (three- to five-second inhale, three- to five-second exhale)
- Expressing gratitude and writing in your journal about it
- Acquiring adequate hydration (sorry, wine and caffeinated beverages don't count)
- Practicing positive thinking
- Consuming high-quality multi-vitamins, probiotics, and omega-3s

THE MASLOW-BLOOM COGNITIVE CONNECTION

In education, many times we cannot teach any more or any harder than we already do. We can, however, be more effective in meeting our goal of increasing leadership capacity (competence, confidence, compassion, creativity, and critical thinking) if we understand the "rocket science" behind cognitive capacity and skill development.

In 1943, Dr. Abraham Maslow and his colleagues identified a hierarchy of basic needs that influence a person's ability and motivation to succeed: physiological, safety, relationship, and esteem-related needs.

When these basic needs are met, then the brain has enough cognitive energy, or battery charge, to devote to creative, critical thinking and academic achievement. Maslow referred to this critical thinking potential as Self-Actualization.

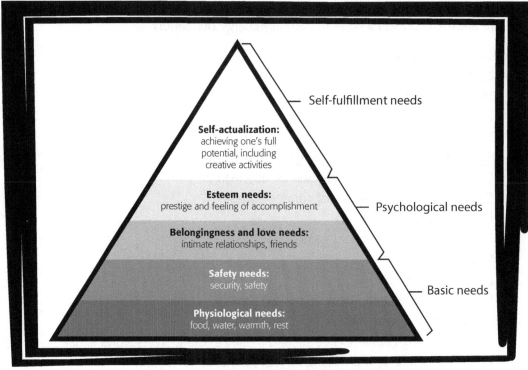

FIGURE 1-1. MASLOW'S HIERARCHY OF NEED

If these needs are not met, the brain becomes stressed and uses tremendous cognitive energy to try to get them met, leaving little energy, or charge, for critical thinking and academic success. Stress drains capacity.

In essence, if the brain is stressed, our creative and critical thinking potential shuts down BECAUSE THERE ISN'T ENOUGH BATTERY POWER TO RUN IT.

Stephen Krashen's "Affective Filter" nailed this connection decades ago, but we didn't yet know the neuroscience behind it. His research concluded that as stress increases, learning decreases. Neurologically speaking, he was 100 percent accurate.

In Maslow's Hierarchy, he refers to critical thinking and creative potential as "Self-Actualization" which equates to Bloom's Taxonomy.

In 1956, Dr. Benjamin Bloom identified six skill levels that are beneficial to learning, critical thinking and retention, known as Bloom's Taxonomy.

The Taxonomy was later updated, but it is still symbolic of the critical thinking and creativity we need to succeed in school and in life.

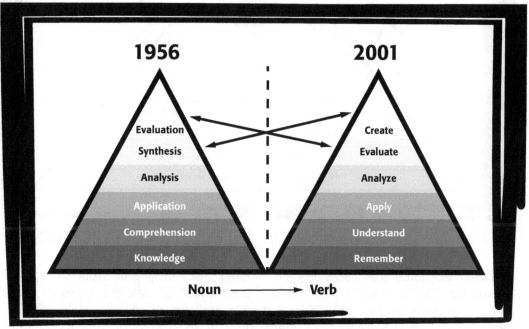

FIGURE 1-2. BLOOM'S TAXONOMY—THEN AND NOW

These critical thinking skills require tremendous cognitive energy to develop, and if too much energy is drained because the Maslow needs are not met, then Bloom skills often go undeveloped.

This is a major reason why many Students who come to us from stressful environments often struggle academically, yet DO NOT improve when placed in academic intervention. They simply don't have the battery charge for it. Meeting Maslow needs provides the foundation to develop the Bloom's academic skill set as noted in Figure 1-3.

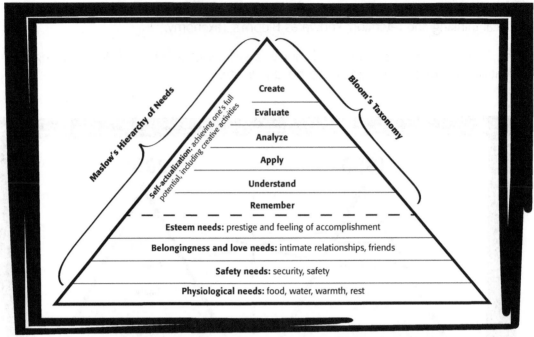

FIGURE 1-3. MASLOW'S HIERARCHY OF NEEDS AND BLOOM'S TAXONOMY

It should be noted that many equate Bloom's Taxonomy with Webb's Depth of Knowledge (DOK). Bloom's refers to the classification of different levels of critical thinking, creativity, and cognitive rigor that increase levels of success, while DOK is a model to analyze and assess how deeply students must think to complete different tasks. This book is focused on developing critical thinking capacity, or the ability to think critically, and that is why we reference Bloom's Taxonomy.

HOW CAN A SCHOOL SYSTEM SYSTEMATICALLY DEVELOP THE 5CS OF LEADERSHIP?

This question is both simple, yet complicated.

Simply stated, we strategically use our resources to get our Student/Parent/Staff batteries #FULLYCHARGED.

The complex component of this task is to first categorize and then assess our Student/Parent/Staff Maslow and Bloom needs and provide the appropriate resources and support. Then, we develop competence, confidence, and compassion by meeting their Maslow needs, and then we develop critical thinking and creativity by meeting their Bloom needs.

Sometimes in a school system, we force-feed curricula and academic intervention to try to help struggling Students, with little to no success. Many have drained batteries due to their Maslow deficiencies, so Bloom interventions are ineffective at that time.

Think of it this way. Let's say you're trying to cut up a steak, but instead of a steak knife, you're provided a straw. When that doesn't work, you're provided another straw and then another, with no success. You can be provided a dozen straws (or academic interventions), but if it's not what you need, no amount provided will solve your problem. In other words, when we force-feed Bloom and neglect Maslow needs, not only does it increase frustration, but it also wastes resources in our ecosystem. That's why identifying, categorizing, and assessing both Maslow and Bloom needs in all three populations is so valuable.

Paying attention to neuroscience increases our efficiency, because it provides the "why" and understanding we need to maximize our ecosystem. And in many instances, to grow Bloom's, we have to cultivate Maslow's.

This sadly only became apparent to me after I (Julie) worked in education for several years.

Science suggests that we would often be more effective if we addressed the root issue of struggle, which is more often a Maslow issue, rather than a Bloom.

> "Kids who are loved at home come to school to learn, and kids who aren't come to school to be loved."
>
> —Nicholas A. Ferroni

Our Maslow needs—healthy food, rest, clothing, security, acceptance, positive relationships, and a series of small successes—are what our brains crave first, and when they are met, our batteries are #FULLYCHARGED.

A drained battery often causes anxiety, depression, and disease, and neurologically shuts down our ability to be creative problem-solvers.

We sometimes make the same mistake when working with Parents and Staff, when we fail to recognize that their batteries might be drained, making it virtually impossible for them to strengthen and charge Student batteries.

School culture that is designed to meet our Student/Parent/Staff Maslow AND Bloom needs strengthens and equips EVERY person in our system with the 5Cs of Leadership, which is the ULTIMATE goal of our educational system.

LET'S TALK ABOUT S.E.X.

When Maslow needs are met, the brain achieves S.E.X., or social-emotional ecstasy.

Social-emotional ecstasy is a positive and powerful brain state in which feel-good hormones and chemicals—such as glutamate, oxytocin, dopamine, serotonin, and norepinephrine—are in proper proportion.

These compounds provide an emotional well-being and positive battery charge, essential to having the competence, confidence, and compassion we need to pursue critical thinking and creativity.

In other words, for a culture to be successful in growing leadership, we need to create conditions where social-emotional ecstasy is our first goal.

I was guilty of not understanding this principle with my student, Brian. He came from a stressful home and struggled with reading and writing, and I spent many months unsuccessfully nagging and cajoling him into doing more of both. I tried to convince him that his success and happiness would increase when his reading and writing improved.

In other words, I was force-feeding his Bloom, but starving his Maslow, so his skills did not improve much.

Don't get me wrong, I was encouraging and polite to him, but I never really put forth the effort to develop a trusting, safe, and positive relationship with him. I labeled him lazy and combative, and I embarrassingly treated him as so.

To charge his drained battery, he really needed to feel safe and accepted. I increased his Maslow stress by not meeting those needs AND increased Bloom stress by forcing more reading and writing. My solution was the opposite of what he needed, so every time he saw me, his stress, or Affective Filter, increased, so I further drained his battery, not charged it.

What does a young brain do when it is stressed? It acts out or zones out. Brian demonstrated this principle often. Instead of growing furious, I should have been curious as to the root of his behavior, and made an adjustment in how I supported him.

I was slowly pulling the pin out of his grenade.

ARE YOU A DRAINER OR A CHARGER?

Environment influences feelings and feelings influence behavior. If Student/Parent/Staff behavior is negative, it's often the result of a negative environment.

How can we decrease environmental factors that cause stress? First, we have to accurately identify the stressors. Nearly all stressors within a school system can be placed into two categories: Maslow and Bloom.

What's next? We maximize our energy and resources by working to decrease or eliminate the stressors accordingly.

But sometimes, we do the opposite because when we encounter someone who is stressed, our interactions or expectations increase their stress. Think of the previous example: "We sometimes force-feed Bloom and neglect Maslow." In schools, we have witnessed far too many times when we have increased stress by increasing the stressors on our Students/Parents/Staff.

If a Student is stressed, fidgety, and can't sit still during reading time, we often take away his recess.

If a Parent is stressed, angry, and arguing, we often argue right back.

If a Staff member is stressed and struggling with classroom management and is told to decrease referrals, we often give a warning or place him on an improvement plan, without training or mentoring.

In each of these situations, the problem was not solved because stress was INCREASED, not DECREASED.

For too long, many of our educational systems increased stress. It may have worked for a while because other environmental stressors were reportedly lower decades ago. But now, our environment is chronically stressful, so many Students/Parents/Staff are regularly coming into our system with drained batteries and looking for help. As a result, our school systems need to adjust and decrease stress to increase battery charge for success.

Think of someone in your school system who is a chronic drainer. Why do you think he behaves in that manner? Is he lacking in a Maslow or Bloom area that prompts battery-draining behavior?

Now think of a skilled charger in your school system. Why do you think he developed that effective skill, and how can it be replicated in the ecosystem?

How can we increase the chargers (producers) in our ecosystem and decrease the stressed drainers (consumers) that absorb all of our resources? We can accomplish this by meeting Maslow and Bloom needs in our Students/Parents/Staff.

What we've learned is: if we can't teach a child to read and write today because he does not have the cognitive capacity to devote to Bloom skills instruction, then we can care for him and encourage him today, so maybe he is cognitively ready and charged up enough to learn to read and write tomorrow.

EVEN THE DOCTORS AGREE

Dr. John Medina explains how Maslow stress directly impacts Bloom abilities in his book, *Brain Rules*:

"I have firsthand experience with the effects of stress on grades. I was a senior in high school when my mother was diagnosed with the disease that would eventually kill her. She had come home late from a doctor's visit and was attempting to fix the family dinner. But when I found her, she was just staring at the kitchen wall. She haltingly related the terminal nature of her medical condition and then, as if that weren't enough, unloaded another bombshell.

My dad, who had some prior knowledge of my Mom's condition, was not handling the news very well and had decided to file for divorce. I felt as if I had just been punched in the stomach. For a few seconds, I could not move.

School the next day and for the next 13 weeks, was a disaster. I don't remember much of the lectures. I only remember staring at my textbooks, thinking about this amazing woman who had taught me to read and love such books, how we used to have a happy family, and that it was all coming to an end. What she must have been feeling, much worse than I would fathom, she never related.

Not knowing how to react, my friends soon withdrew from me as I withdrew from them. I lost the ability to concentrate, my mind wandering back to my childhood.

My academic effort became a train wreck. I got the only D I would ever get in my school career, and I couldn't have cared less.

Even after all these years, it is still tough to write about that high school moment. But it easily illustrates this second, very powerful consequence of stress, underscoring with sad vengeance our Brain Rule: Stressed brains do not learn the same way as non-stressed brains.

My grief at least had an endpoint. Imagine growing up in an emotionally unstable home, where stress seems never-ending.

Given that stress can powerfully affect learning, one might predict that children living in high-anxiety households would not perform as well academically as kids living in more nurturing households.

That is exactly what researchers have found.

Marital stress at home can negatively affect academic performance in almost every way measurable, and at nearly every age. Initial studies focused on grade-point averages over time. They reveal striking disparities of achievement between divorce and control groups.

Subsequent investigations showed though that even when a couple stays together, children living in emotionally unstable homes get lower grades…it was the presence of overt conflict or stress, not divorce, that predicted grade failure…

The stronger the degree of conflict, the greater the effect on performance" (184-185).

DISTRESS SHUTS DOWN S.E.X.

There are two types of stress: eustress and distress.

Eustress is a positive stress. It's a combination of anxiety and excitement, which can charge us up and help us to perform at higher levels by "firing on all cylinders." We might feel this way if we are buying a house, making a sales pitch, or training for a marathon.

Distress is when anxiety far outweighs other emotions, and we feel threatened. This negative stress drains our capacity.

Distress decreases those happy, feel-good chemicals, which promote social-emotional ecstasy and learning and increases cortisol, a chemical that becomes toxic at high levels, which decreases learning.

To maximize the efficiency and productivity in our schools' ecosystems, our goal then is to decrease distress and increase social-emotional ecstasy so we grow the capacity to strengthen, encourage, and care for others.

OUR MIND CONTROLS OUR BRAIN AND BODY

Our mind, comprised of our thoughts and feelings, controls our brain and body.

If someone or something threatens to attack, our mind feels fear, which triggers our fight/flight/freeze amygdala, or the extreme emotional processing center of our brain that is responsible for survival instincts. There are actually two amygdalae, one in each hemisphere of the brain, though they're often referred to in the singular: amygdala. Our brain then sends signals to our body to release chemicals, such as adrenaline and cortisol, to help us react quickly and efficiently in order to escape the threat.

Adrenaline increases our heart rate and short-term energy bursts. Cortisol increases glucose in our bloodstream, which is helpful for a quick energy boost, and it regulates blood pressure during the fight/flight/freeze response.

PHYSICALLY

- PUPILS DILATE
- SALIVA DECREASES
- SHALLOW BREATHING UTILIZED
- HEART RATE INCREASES
- MUSCLES TENSE AND TWITCH
- CORTISOL INCREASES
- IMMUNITY DECREASES

COGNITIVELY AND EMOTIONALLY

- ANXIETY AND FEAR INCREASE
- IMPAIRED CONCENTRATION
- DECREASED RETENTION
- CONFUSION
- INDECISION
- MENTAL PARALYSIS AND CRITICAL THINKING CAPACITY DIMINISHES
- ACUTE DISTRESS

FIGURE 1-4. FIGHT/FLIGHT/FREEZE

This is a brilliant and efficient short-term survival response that has increased our survival throughout the centuries. Once a perceived threat has passed, these chemicals return to a normal level, and our body systems start to function regularly again.

But what happens when the threat never goes away and we FEEL continual fear? In other words, what if our environment is continually full of perceived imminent threats and/or our choices increase our threat perceptions?

Cortisol, though helpful in immediate threatening situations, drains battery capacity and eventually slows down non-essential fight/flight/freeze mechanisms such as our digestive, reproductive, and metabolic systems, and healthy developmental and growth processes.

Many health professionals have labeled cortisol as public health enemy #1. Too much cortisol for too long causes tremendous inflammation throughout the body, which decreases oxygen-rich blood flow to the brain, gray matter growth, and neural connections. Body systems are also hampered due to detrimental impacts on immunity, sleep, concentration, memory, emotional regulation, and hormonal balances.

BATTLING GOLIATH

Nowadays, many of us are dealing with sustained stress due to work, family, health, scheduling, finances, and many other issues. In addition, our environmental choices also increase our threat perception because many of our choices end up acting as stressors and further drain our batteries.

Our brains and bodies become stressed when we have too little:
- Sleep
- Exercise
- Healthy food
- Positive face-to-face relationships and acceptance

And we CHOOSE too much:
- Social media
- Violent video-gaming
- Binge TV-watching

Deprivation of the good stuff and bingeing on the harmful stuff causes a stressed, drained brain and body.

Don't believe it?

What are the most diagnosed health issues around the world?
- Hypertension
- Obesity
- Heart disease
- Cancer
- Anxiety
- Depression

According to the Centers for Disease Control and Prevention, these are considered stress-induced conditions, and our Students/Parents/Staff are being diagnosed with them at an alarming rate.

Our Students are the post-9/11 generation who have never known a world without terrorism, economic uncertainty, standardized testing, school shootings, reality TV, and constant social media comparisons.

Dr. Janis Whitlock, the Director of the Cornell Research Program on Self-Injury and Recovery, states: "If we wanted to create an environment that churned out 'angsty' people, we have done it." Though family and school stress contribute significantly, "… our children are in a cauldron of stimulus they CAN'T get away from, or don't WANT to get away from, or don't know HOW to get away from."

In our current society, educators are battling a Goliath like never before, and that enemy is STRESS. Stress drains our battery, and makes it difficult to be a leader who cares for and grows capacity in others.

We are standing firm and calling for an all-out WAR against unnecessary stress in our school ecosystems. Though this is a lofty goal, we can at least serve as a positive and caring support system to help our Students/Parents/Staff manage stress more effectively.

We challenge your school system to analyze and eliminate unnecessary stressors and increase the positivity and encouragement provided to stakeholders. When we identify and meet Maslow and Bloom needs, our schools can be a place that people want to get into (instead of run to get out of) and we can compete with Disneyland for the title "The Happiest Place on Earth."

Why is that an important goal? Because it has a #FULLYCHARGED effect!

CALL TO ACTION

This book is not a negative critique of society. It's an empowering manual that has two sections: one devoted to increasing social-emotional ecstasy (S.E.X.), with chapters on meeting the Maslow needs of our Students/Parents/Staff, and one section devoted to SKILLS, with chapters designed to increase Bloom's critical thinking and creativity in our Students/Parents/Staff.

In each chapter, we share Narratives, Rocket Science Research and Resources, and "Battery Charging" Strategies. There are also Book Study/Twitter Chat questions and a vlog (video-blog) with us as we briefly discuss our thoughts about each chapter. To continue to grow these ideas, we have also developed a 21 Day #FULLYCHARGED Challenge that we encourage you to participate in to recharge your brain for success. We hope this blend is beneficial in providing insight into designing a leadership-cultivating environment that ALL want to be included.

It's not about the role or title of "leader" that we are focused on developing, but rather the capacity, or competence, confidence, compassion, and creative, critical thinking it takes to strengthen, encourage, and care for ourselves and others.

*   *   *   *   *

To accomplish #FULLYCHARGED capacity,
we must be able to say YES to these two questions:

GOT S.E.X.?
GOT SKILLS?

#FULLYCHARGED

CHAPTER 1: BOOK STUDY/TWITTER CHAT QUESTIONS

1. How do the 5Cs of Leadership (competence, confidence, compassion, creativity, critical thinking) influence leadership capacity?

2. How charged is your battery when you wake up on an average school day?

3. If you're not #FULLYCHARGED, which changes can you make?

4. Discuss the Maslow-Bloom cognitive connection.

5. Identify three ideas that resonate with you from this chapter. How will you share those ideas with your Students/Parents/Staff?

Please visit effectiveteachingpd.com or mbsimplesolution.com to watch the #FULLYCHARGED Author Chat about this chapter and participate in our 21 Day Challenge.

SECTION I
Got S.E.X.?

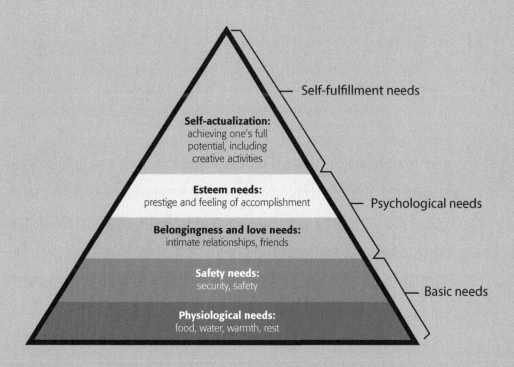

Self-fulfillment needs

Self-actualization:
achieving one's full
potential, including
creative activities

Esteem needs:
prestige and feeling of accomplishment

Psychological needs

Belongingness and love needs:
intimate relationships, friends

Safety needs:
security, safety

Basic needs

Physiological needs:
food, water, warmth, rest

CHAPTER 2
Meeting Student Maslow Needs

"How powerful would our world be if we raised kids not afraid to take risks, who were not afraid to think, and who had a champion? Every child deserves a champion, an adult who will never give up on them, who understands the power of connection and insists they become the best they can possibly be. Is this job tough? You betcha. But it is NOT impossible. We can do this; we're educators. We're born to make a difference."

—Rita Pierson

"Sometimes we are looking for a giant 'AHA' or light bulb-flashing Bloom breakthrough moment, and when we don't get it, we think we failed."

—Julie Adams

What happened to Brian, my former Maslow and Bloom stressed Student?

A few years ago, I (Julie) ran into him at a restaurant. I was there eating with a group of people and a large young man called out as he walked toward me, "Yo, Mrs. Adams? Is that you?"

As he got closer, I admit that my fight/flight/freeze mechanism was triggered when I recognized him. It was Brian. Brian was the ONE Student in whom I truly felt I had failed, and his temper had been unleashed on me many times before.

I didn't know whether to prepare for a battle or a bear hug.

"Mrs. Adams, do you remember me? Brian? I was in your eighth grade class many years ago. I saw you and wanted to come over here and tell you a few things that I think about your teaching."

On his last day of eighth grade, I clearly remember watching him walk out my classroom door for the last time, thinking to myself that I have failed that child. I never saw him smile, nor was I successful in helping him develop the academic (or behavioral) skills he lacked.

I later heard that he had dropped out of high school after someone "pulled his pin" and he unleashed a grenade of violence on another Student, which resulted in his expulsion. I prayed that he would find the comfort and peace that his young heart craved.

"Brian, it is so good to see you! What have you been up to?" I tried to be enthusiastic, but was filled with trepidation as I waited for his response.

"Well, you probably heard that I dropped out of high school? That's true. I also got into a nasty bar fight and spent a few months in the county jail. Thankfully, the charges were dropped, so I enrolled in the military. Yep, I did a couple of tours in Iraq and Afghanistan as a front-line medic and helped save many lives. That was some dangerous stuff, for sure."

"Wow, Brian, I had no idea! That's very brave and admirable of you."

"Some might say that, Mrs. Adams, but I felt that I needed to redeem myself after treating others poorly for so long. I wanted to tell you that I'm sorry for

the trouble I caused you while I was your Student and that everything has turned out OK for me. I've been married for a few years now and we are expecting our first child. I'm an assistant manager at a large store, and we're doing pretty good. I try to help out other troubled kids and wounded veterans as much as I can. It makes me feel good."

"Wow, I had no idea; that's fantastic! I'm so happy for you, Brian."

"I still want to tell you a few things though, Mrs. Adams."

"Of course, Brian."

"Well, for starters, I hated you—or thought I did. I couldn't handle the attention and help you tried to give me, and I didn't know how to deal with all the junk that was going on at home. I was ashamed of what I came from, and I was afraid you would think less of me, so I pushed you away as much as possible. You expected so much from me, and I just couldn't do it, so I fought against you."

"I'm so sorry, Brian. I've often felt that I failed you. I just couldn't figure out how to help you be successful. I thought you needed more practice with reading and writing, so I forced that on you. You probably needed so many other things, and I didn't provide them."

"But that's just it, Mrs. Adams. I wouldn't have accepted anything else even if you had provided it because I couldn't receive anything at that time. It's like my brain couldn't, or wouldn't, handle it. But I want to tell you something that I have never told anyone else… you saved my life."

"What do you mean?"

"One day I was absent and the next day when I went to school, there you were standing at your door, smiling and greeting each of us as we entered. When you got to me, you said, "Hey there, Brian, where were you yesterday? I missed you, and I'm so glad you're here!" I don't think I even responded to you because what you said caught me off guard. You see, I was absent the day before because I tried to commit suicide, and just like everything else at that time, I failed at it. I told myself that if anyone noticed that I had been absent, then I wouldn't ever try to hurt myself again. It's like you were put there for a reason because not only did you mention it, but then you said, "I'm so glad you're here!" Nobody had ever said that to me before. Nobody."

At this point, we both had tears in our eyes as we looked at each other.

"Brian, I had no idea. Thank you for telling me. I've always thought that I had completely failed you."

"Mrs. Adams, if you ever question whether or not you make a difference as an educator, I'm living proof and here to tell you that you are a game-changer. Even when I couldn't accept your help, you continued to offer it. You pursued me and pushed me to succeed, even when I pushed you away. You were THE ONE who made the difference. I now realize that you made me uncomfortable because you paid attention to me, when others didn't. I strangely craved your attention, though I fought against it. I'm here today to tell you thank you. I now use so many of your reading and writing strategies because they make sense now, and I have to do a lot of reading and writing for my job. It is not a coincidence that I was in your class that year. It's the little things that you do EVERY DAY that matter."

I continued thinking about what he said as I drove home that night, "It's the little things that you do EVERY DAY that matter."

Students who need their Maslow needs met often ask for it in the most unloving and uncomfortable of ways. Sometimes we are looking for a giant "A-HA" or light bulb-flashing Bloom breakthrough moment, and when we don't get it, we think we failed. His academic skills did improve a little over the course of the year, but I was often frustrated with him because I thought he just wasn't putting in the effort for more improvement. I now realize that he didn't have enough battery charge at that time; however, later, he did have enough capacity, and he was able to use them.

Brian reminded me that it's the little things that we do every day that matter most to many of our Students/Parents/Staff, and those little things are far more important than a test score.

"People will forget what you said, forget what you did, but they will never forget how you made them feel."

—Maya Angelou

"In agriculture, if you plant a seed and it does not flourish, you do not blame the seed; you blame the environment."

—PJ Caposey

Jameson was 11 years old and a great kid. A model Student, leader, and decorated athlete, the only trouble he had ever been in was once having his behavior card flipped in Kindergarten (discussing that negative Maslow practice would take a whole different book).

Jameson's father, with whom he is very close, was diagnosed with cancer around Christmas time, and his father's treatment involved being in isolation and away from the family for several weeks. During this time, Jameson was the aggressor in a physical confrontation with two other Students at school. Oddly, these two were his friends and even part of his birthday celebration just weeks earlier.

Jackson was a 10-year-old, straight-A Student, who absolutely LOVED school. He was very social and frequently received friendly reminders to quiet down, but was a shining star and delight to be around. During the final quarter of the school year, his work completion rate plummeted, and so did his grades.

His Parents, being involved and concerned, contacted the school and asked for the Counselor to meet with him. It turned out that the impending move of Jackson's birth mom back into the area was causing a great deal of tension and stress for him. He adored both his birth mom and current living situation with his dad and stepmom, but was concerned how the new dynamic would work. His schoolwork, as a result, suffered the impact of this stress.

In both of these situations, it was fairly easy to identify the reasons for otherwise "great" kids suddenly making choices that negatively impacted their social and academic success.

Jameson needed to talk with someone he trusted and get a little extra support during his dad's treatment. As soon as that was provided and his dad returned home, things started to normalize.

Jackson talked through the problem with his Counselor and, upon the transition, he noticed that everything went perfectly. His fears did not come to fruition, and he ended up with the best of both worlds, having all of his parents centrally located around him.

In both cases, the school was a central part of the solution, and everyone involved "understood" the circumstances and wanted to help. Not only were these problems easy to identify, it was easy to sympathize, empathize, and provide support.

In essence, this is exactly what schools are designed to do, and WE are often great at it. When short-term stress happens in our Students' lives, we problem-solve, collaborate, and do whatever it takes to help. And we (almost) NEVER blame the child.

Providing support in the short-term to my (PJ) own two kids, Jameson and Jackson, is different, and maybe even easier, than providing support to kids who suffer from long-term adverse environments like my other children, my Students, like Tyrone.

Tyrone was one of my favorite Students. He was brooding, occasionally angry and defiant, yet incredibly charming and protective. What complicated things for Tyrone was that he was a 16-year-old child wrapped up in a 6 foot 3 inch, 240-pound mountain of muscle.

Tyrone had never met his father, rarely saw his mother, and was essentially responsible for raising his three siblings. He was all things to all people, with nothing left over for himself.

His tantrums and acts of defiance were intimidating to everyone, including adults. He did not feel safe anywhere, as he grew up and lived in an environment where fighting was the norm and an unfortunate rite of passage for adolescent males. He would often share with me that when a conflict arose, which was often, people would tell him that because he was too big to fight, they would just have to shoot him.

Tyrone never felt safe.

This all contributed to his toxic and defiant behavior toward adults. He cared little about his schoolwork, and his work ethic was constantly questioned because he did not leverage his enormous physical size and talent to the advantage of the school's athletic programs. He was stuck, angry, and drained. Unfortunately, none of this was his fault.

In education, we are often skilled in helping Students navigate a single traumatic incident that negatively influences their behavior in the short term. However, we sometimes need to increase our response when serving Students who have suffered a myriad of traumatic incidents that have perpetuated long-term negative behavior.

Remember in agriculture, if a seed is planted and it does not flourish, the seed is not blamed, but the environment. Sometimes in education though, we blame the "seed" even when the environment has been less than fertile.

Our hope is that we cultivate an environment that grows successful Students— ALL Students. Not just the ones who come from good environments.

They all deserve it, and our society needs it.

"We knew if she did not receive the support she needed,
the learning gaps would increase."

—Rosa Isiah

I (Rosa) met Jenny when she was a sweet third-grader with a great sense of humor and dynamic personality. She was a leader in her classroom and enjoyed receiving positive praise from her teacher and peers. A strong communicator who was able to identify and describe her worries and frustration, she used a number of mindful calming strategies learned from her school counselor when frustrated. However, this wasn't always the case for Jenny.

She enrolled at Lincoln Elementary as a first-grade Student, and even then she stood out from her peers in a number of ways. She sought constant attention, both positive and negative, from her teacher and peers. She didn't even mind the negative attention, as long as she had a captive audience.

Jenny threw tantrums when she didn't get her way and often lashed out at her peers, biting or hitting. Her teacher established a strong relationship with her, and attempted a number of behavioral classroom interventions, but her behavior didn't improve and her academic progress was limited. The school's Response to Intervention team scheduled a support meeting with Jenny's caregiver. We knew that if she did not receive the support she needed, the learning gap would continue to increase.

After meeting with her uncle, we learned that Jenny experienced a great deal of trauma prior to enrolling in school. She was taken from her parent as a baby; her mother struggled with substance abuse and was forced to give up her children. Jenny was passed around from family member to family member until her uncle decided to adopt her. Though her home life improved somewhat, she still dealt with a number of issues, and she lacked stability. We knew that we needed to support her Maslow before we could address her Bloom.

We connected Jenny to both inside and outside of school counseling services and utilized trauma-impacted strategies to calm her when she became stressed. Her caregivers also agreed to family counseling and using similar strategies at home with her. At school, she was included in a "friendship" group designed to address her social-emotional needs, and she met with her counselor once a week and whenever else she needed immediate support. Within a few weeks, her teacher and peers began to see many positive changes. Jenny and her family were in the process of acquiring the tools necessary to meet her Maslow *needs and charge up her battery. As a result, she was able to now receive and benefit from the Bloom support she needed. When we partnered with her family and supported the whole child, Jenny bloomed!*

Many of our Students have experienced Adverse Childhood Experiences (ACEs) and are living with trauma-impacted brains. Physical and verbal abuse, poverty, domestic abuse, and neglect all result in trauma. Trauma highly impacts a child's brain development, essentially disrupting the ability to learn and focus. Trauma impacted Students often seek attention, any type of attention, making choices that result in negative behavior. We often label those Students as impatient, disengaged, and defiant. We may do this due to our lack of knowledge, or our frustration from limited access to resources. Trauma-impacted Students are living in a constant state of fight/flight/freeze, and this stressed state shuts down Bloom learning.

We've all had Jennies in our classrooms. It is important for educators to understand the effects of trauma on the brain in order to implement trauma-informed policies and practices in our schools. The effects of Adverse Childhood Experiences have long-term educational implications resulting in learning gaps and learning loss. When we fail to address basic needs, especially for ACEs-impacted Students, we fail as educators.

To grow Bloom's, cultivate Maslow's.

ROCKET SCIENCE RESEARCH

Here are four concepts we want to convey about the young brain:
- The young brain is different.
- The young brain, as a result of these differences, is very susceptible to experiencing high levels of stress.
- Chronic stress negatively impacts the brain and shuts down learning, and an increasing number of our Students are suffering.
- Student success is not by chance, but by design.

As educators, we need to be particularly skilled in cultivating social-emotional ecstasy, and designing an environment that minimizes stress and maximizes cognitive battery charge.

IDENTIFYING NEED IS NOT ENOUGH

Do you remember sitting in your educational theory class and learning about Maslow's Hierarchy of Needs? We do. In fact, it is one of the few things that seemingly every new teacher candidate takes with them from education courses.

As a Superintendent, PJ has witnessed in teacher interview after interview, that Student Maslow needs are often mentioned by a candidate, and when probing questions are asked, most can identify that Students need to feel safe and have basic needs met in order to learn effectively in their class.

The issue is that we often stop right there at the "identify" stage. As educators, we are often equipped to "manage" a few stressed Students whose primary focus is on survival. We see evidence in class that these Students may not be interested, or even capable of, learning algebra or the differences between a dependent and independent clause. It is important to recognize that a young, stressed brain innately acts out or zones out, as a survival mechanism due to limited cognitive energy.

In the past, educators would think about, prepare, and make adjustments for the special needs of these few kids. But in the last few decades, the amount of these Students has increased as sleep, exercise, healthy food, and positive face-to-face relationship deprivations are now commonplace in our stressed society.

Our educational systems are often not prepared for the sheer number of these stressed kids in our schools and the negative ways in which they behave. More importantly, many educators are simply not educated in how stress actually decreases Students' skills, brain development and neuroplasticity, and as a result, our patience sometimes runs low when working with them.

We are not saying the young brain is not as capable as it was in previous decades. In fact, it may be more capable as we now have more research and understanding about growing capacity.

However, the young brain, especially when stressed, does require certain elements to be successful. Our educational system must provide these elements AND provide more education about them.

THE YOUNG BRAIN IS DIFFERENT

The young brain is different, and it is HIGHLY influenced by environment.

In the last 20 years, neuroscientists have discovered far more differences in the young brain due to fancy neuroimaging tools such as Functional Magnetic Resonance Imaging (fMRI), Positron Emission Tomography Scans (PET) and Quantitative Electroencephalography (qEEG).

It was long believed that the brain was fully developed around age 12, and if a child had not developed a skill set by then, he probably would not. The old adage, *you can't teach an old dog new tricks,* was a popular sentiment. But scientists now know that is not true!

NEUROPLASTICITY—THE POWER OF PLASTIC

Our brains have neuroplasticity, which is a sponginess or stretchy plastic factor, which provides the ability to grow and change throughout life in response to EVERY experience.

There are certain times in our lives when we have tremendous neuroplasticity, or the ability to form new neural connections and skills. Neuroscientists have concluded that the young brain is under major construction until approximately 25, not 12, and it has extreme levels of neuroplasticity during this time.

Abilities are not "set in stone" in early adolescence as previously believed. Brains are more malleable during youth (ages 0 to 25) than at any other time, due to large amounts of gray matter production.

Dr. Frances Jensen, author of *The Teenage Brain*, explains how the adolescent brain is a paradox; it is extremely powerful yet vulnerable. "It has an overabundance of gray matter (the neurons that form the basic building blocks of the brain) and an undersupply of white matter (the connective wiring that helps information flow efficiently from one part of the brain to the other)" (26).

This is why neuroscientists often refer to the young brain as a brand new, powerful sports car with only one flaw…it has no brakes.

PORCELAIN OR PLAY-DOH?

The discovery of neuroplasticity is GREAT news for educators because it validates the research that proves that WHAT WE DO MATTERS! High-performing teachers can overcome the deficiencies of low-performing Students almost every single time.

In other words, if Students are not born with an innate trait, then we can till the skill.

Think how powerful this concept is! If Students are not born with the ability to control their emotions or impulses, organize their math binder, write a persuasive paragraph or load the dishwasher correctly, we can grow their capacity by providing explicit instruction because their skill set is not like porcelain, but Play-Doh.

If a Student comes to us underperforming, we can provide the environment that will foster the development of new neural pathways, because these pathways are begging for constant connection and growth!

However, in order to overcome Student deficiencies, it is beneficial to understand how the young brain differs and what it requires to be successful and then include those elements in the learning environment.

Tilling the skill is more effective when stress is low and the brain is in a positive state of social-emotional ecstasy (or S.E.X.), which provides enough cognitive capacity and battery charge, for new skill development.

AVOID COMMITTING ASSUMICIDE

Sometimes, we put the same expectations on the young brain that we have for the mature brain, and we essentially set a child up for failure. Or we commit assumicide and assume that if a child is of a certain age, he should have a certain skill, such as knowing how to organize an essay, iron a shirt, or have a respectful, face-to-face conversation with an adult.

Brain age and size, though, do not guarantee skill development. For example, imagine that twins are born, and one is raised alone in a dark closet with zero engagement and the other is raised in a "normal" environment with social interaction, school, nature, music, art, travel, technology, and so forth. At ages 8, 10, 15, both of their brains will be the same age and nearly the same size, but they will have developed very different neural pathways and skill sets.

Skills are often developed when there is an emotional connection, analysis, repetition, AND reflection of an experience. So if a child has not engaged in all those ways with an experience, then he may not acquire a skill set, even if he's had the experience. It's even far more unlikely for him to have a skill set if he has never had the experience. Yet we often hold Students accountable for a skill based on their age, not experience.

IT'S NOT JUST THEIR OVERACTIVE HORMONES

How many times have you heard a child's irrational behavior blamed on his hormones?

Neuroscientist Jay Giedd from the National Institute of Mental Health, shared helpful insight into the young brain in the PBS special, *Inside the Teenage Brain*, and other doctors have also written extensively on this topic: Jane Healy, Eric Jensen, Judy Willis, and Frances Jensen, to name a few. Their research concludes that the young brain acts differently not just because hormones are over-stimulated, but because the brain is both UNDER AND OVER active in certain regions until the mid-20s. If it were just their hormones, then we could not influence their behavior and skills. But it's not.

The brain develops from the stem forward, and the last part of the brain to develop is called the pre-frontal cortex. This area is also referred to as the executive functioning center, and it is in charge of many skills including: cause and effect analysis, emotional regulation, impulse control, organizational skills, and rational decision-making.

Neuroscientists believe this area does not fully activate in many until age 25, not 12.

Car insurance companies have known this for decades and revised their policies as a result. They charge more to insure young drivers because young drivers are 300 percent more likely to engage in risky, dangerous driving.

Wait! What? The young brain is more likely to engage in risky, dangerous behavior and, therefore, should be treated differently? Neuroscientists say YES.

This means that car insurance companies pay attention to research when making decisions about their clients, but educators often do not.

When we ask young Johnny why he made a bad choice, 9 times out of 10 he will say, "I DON'T KNOW!" We think he is being defiant, but he's not. He's being brutally honest and insightful about his brain development, or lack thereof.

We commit assumicide when we think a child can manage his causal connections, emotions, impulses, and make rational decisions at age 10, 14, or even 20 years of age. Unfortunately, this means we have ignored the volumes of research that show, in many circumstances, he does not have the cognitive capacity yet to do so.

Many of the behaviors exhibited by the young brain that frustrate adults are all associated with an immature pre-frontal cortex:
- Poor judgment
- Overly emotional and dramatic responses
- Incessant fidgeting
- Paranoid, *nobody likes me, everybody hates me*, mentality
- Obnoxious outbursts that lack an appropriateness filter

- Messy and disorganized tendencies
- Hyper or hypo activity

What do we often do when a Student says, "I DON'T KNOW!" after making a bad choice? We punish, instead of tilling the skill.

This misunderstood punishment often increases stress in the young brain, which increases frustration and negative behavior, and when it occurs often, we incorrectly label the Student as deviant and initiate a downward spiral.

Students are often not insubordinate, but ignorant of our expectation, due to their underdeveloped pre-frontal cortex.

Just as we provide explicit instruction in solving an algorithm, when we provide explicit instruction in the executive functioning skills, we greatly increase Student success because we till the skill and enhance neural connections that increase both their emotional and academic intelligence.

WHY YOUR NOODLE NEEDS PRACTICE

Keith Blanchard, author of *Your Brain: The Art, Magic, and Science of What Makes You You*, provides this summary of our brain:

> *"The four key components of your neurological system are neurons, axons, synapses, and dendrites. Neurons are like little trees, with multiple outstretched branches called dendrites and a single long trunk called an axon. The axon communicates information to other neurons' dendrites. The junctions between the axon of one neuron and the dendrite of another are called synapses, and it's across these tiny gaps, the synaptic cleft, that communication takes place" (4).*

Neurotransmitters such as glutamate, gaba, oxytocin, dopamine, serotonin, and endorphins communicate information from synapse to synapse. Too little or too much of these chemicals can wreak havoc in the transmission process.

Research encourages us to provide calm and consistent, explicit instruction, and deliberate practice of a specific skill to promote dendritic and synaptic connections. Repetition and explicit instruction are key when it comes to tilling skill. Every time we learn something new, our brain creates a pathway that tries to connect to another pathway, to strengthen the learning.

The more we learn about and practice the new skill via explicit instruction and deliberate practice, the stronger the pathway becomes, which increases the retention rate.

Explicit instruction sounds and looks like this: *"Students, this is* what *we are doing today,* why *we are doing it, and* how *we are doing it (model). Now let's* practice *together. Now you will receive* descriptive feedback *in case you need to make an adjustment to be more successful. Let's* practice *some more."*

"Practice does NOT make perfect; only perfect practice makes perfect."

—Vince Lombardi

Perfect practice is the result of explanation (especially explaining the WHY), modeling, guided practice, feedback, and continued practice after revision. Perfect practice allows the brain to prune away missteps and inappropriate pathways. This is why providing descriptive feedback and revision opportunities is so valuable to the learning process.

In the article "Three Things to Know About the Teenage Brain," author Julie Baron explains:

"A major finding in research on the developing brain is that it is physically changing shape by undergoing a process of specialization called pruning. Neuron connections from behaviors no longer needed, literally disappear, while others are formed through the engagement in new and more targeted understanding and tasks. This process is facilitated by myelination.

Myelin is a fatty substance that insulates the connections between brain cells, particularly those pathways that are used most often. With frequent use, pathways in the brain become myelinated, creating a faster and more efficient pathway for that task.

This is why when we're learning something new, it's challenging at first. Most of us have to focus on a skill and practice it over and over again until the pathways for that skill become myelinated and the skill becomes easier.

The processes that occur in the frontal lobe of the brain—focus, attention, goal-directed behavior, judgment and problem-solving—combined with the overactive amygdala, create unique challenges for adolescents. DNA, time, and opportunities for practice and learning, allow adaptive neuron pathways to myelinate and strengthen.

Supportive and understanding relationships with adults are a powerful tool in guiding adolescents into maturity while their brains are still fully developing. As adults, the more we provide teens with opportunities to focus, pay attention, practice goal-directed behavior, use good judgment, and solve problems, while understanding that emotions are at play, and mistakes will be made, the better off they'll be."

This neurological concept is helpful in understanding why learning a new skill absorbs cognitive capacity until the skill has become automated, or a neural pathway has been constructed and used enough to become protected by myelin. For most people, a "one and done" learning session is not enough to fully develop a skill set, yet we often utilize this strategy in the classroom.

Some need extensive practice in certain academic AND social-emotional skills such as writing an essay, solving an equation, or controlling their impulses. Their efficient brains may not initially make an emotional connection to the skill and, therefore, will work to eliminate it to conserve energy and space. The more we practice the skill, the more likely it is to stay.

EMOTION DRIVES COGNITION

To increase the likelihood of making new content and skills stick, develop emotion-enticing and attention-getting learning experiences!

Create an emotional learning experience that young brains find enough value in to retain. Incorporate sensory stimulation, prior knowledge, engagement, excitement, interaction, storytelling, real-world application, and FUN emotional connections to new content, and then provide the explicit skills-based instruction, feedback, and practice to increase Student success.

WHAT AREA OF THE YOUNG BRAIN IS OVERACTIVE?

Neuroscientists believe that one of the most active areas in a young developing brain is the amygdala. It is the extreme positive and negative emotional processing center that is directly responsible for survival or fight/flight/freeze mode.

What does this really mean? Nearly all of our Students are operating in fight/flight/ freeze mode, and that has a drastic, and often negative, influence on their behavior and battery capacity.

Neuroscientists have learned that when the amygdala is negatively stimulated or distressed, it becomes flooded with "neural metabolic activity," so new memories and information cannot pass through it to the reasoning and memory storage areas of the brain. Essentially, when Students are distressed, learning shuts down.

Decades ago, linguistics expert, Dr. Stephen Krashen, identified this phenomenon while studying language acquisition. He discovered that negative AFFECT, or emotions and confidence, leads to negative acquisition abilities. As we learned over and over in our teaching credential program, increased stress = decreased learning.

If Student distress levels are high, an Affective Filter in the brain is activated, which limits learning capacity; therefore, acquisition levels are low. Dr. Judy Willis, neurologist and author of *Research-Based Strategies That Ignite Student Learning*, agrees and makes the neurological connection between the two in her book; the Affective Filter IS the amygdala, and it serves as the gatekeeper of learning.

To improve Student success, neuroscientists recommend that educators pay attention to stressors and make adjustments to lower stress in a learning environment.

Stressors can include:
- Boredom
- Being overwhelmed or underwhelmed
- Fatigue
- Hunger
- Sarcasm
- Chaos
- Hypercritical feedback
- Lighting (too bright or too dark)
- Cold calling
- No revision opportunities
- Intimidation, bullying, conflict

In short, an underactive pre-frontal cortex and an overactive amygdala create the perfect storm for distress. This is important to understand because in order for us to reach our goal of helping Students be successful and develop competence, confidence, compassion, creativity, and critical thinking, we must actively work to minimize stress.

THERE IS JUST ONE PROBLEM

This is where a new body of research on Adverse Childhood Experiences (ACEs) provides an opportunity for educators, and hopefully all adults, to confront the brutal facts about Student stress. There are certain types of childhood stressors that are more difficult to overcome.

The study of ACEs began in 1990 by Dr. Vincent Felitti. He discovered that nearly half of his obese patients had suffered some type of adverse experience, such as abuse or neglect, early in life.

Dr. Felitti, Dr. Robert Anda from the Center for Disease Control, and Kaiser Permanente teamed up to analyze 17,000 patients. They were specifically studying two things: 1) the relationship between exposure to abuse and household dysfunction in childhood and the development of adult health-risk behavior (smoking, alcoholism, severe obesity), and 2) the relationship between exposure to abuse and household dysfunction in childhood and the development of disease.

They studied each patient's exposure in three categories (abuse, neglect, household dysfunction) and the following 10 specific areas:
- Physical abuse
- Emotional abuse

- Sexual abuse
- Physical neglect
- Emotional neglect
- Criminal behavior/incarcerated household member
- Divorce or parental separation
- Mental illness
- Substance abuse
- Domestic violence, especially inflicted on the mother

What they found was both common sense and shocking. The common sense is that the more ACEs someone experiences, the more negative the impact is on healthy brain development and long-term health.

What is the shocking conclusion from ACEs research? ACEs are rampant! Nearly 70 percent of the patients had experienced at least one ACE, and 12.6 percent had experienced four or more, and they were twice as likely to develop heart disease and cancer and three and a half times as likely to develop chronic obstructive pulmonary disease.

But even more shocking were the patient demographics. When first reading the results, one might assume the patients were poverty stricken, lacked proper health care, and uneducated in healthy lifestyle choices.

Nope.

The study was conducted in San Diego; nearly 70 percent of the participants were college-educated, employed, middle class, and Caucasian.

The ACEs research proved that trauma in childhood increased long-term health risk factors, regardless of race, socioeconomic status, and access to quality health care.

The 2013 "National Survey of Children's Health" asserts that one third of Students ages 12 to 17, have experienced at least two ACEs! The 2016 survey disaggregates data by state and identifies the state with the lowest incident of ACEs as Minnesota with 38 percent of adults having experienced a traumatic experience as a child, and Arkansas with the highest percentage, a whopping 56 percent!

ACEs AND DELINQUENCY

Fairfax County is becoming a leader in examining how ACEs are impacting the criminal system. The hope is to identify a cause, or root issue, to remediate in hopes of decreasing the need for youth probation and incarceration. As a result, the juvenile court screens all new youth offenders who are placed on probation and then identifies need and provides support.

The statistics are mind-boggling, with 85 percent of juveniles in the probation system having at least one ACE. Our young people are experiencing significant trauma and that trauma, when left untreated, has detrimental impacts on their brains, our schools, and our society.

This is not an urban problem.

This is not a poor problem.

This is an everyone problem.

This is our problem.

This simply reinforces the notion that everyone, EVERYONE, may be fighting a battle we know nothing about.

ACEs IMPACT LONG-TERM HEALTH

Figure 2-1 shows a very telling ACEs pyramid that demonstrates the impacts of ACEs, when left unmitigated.

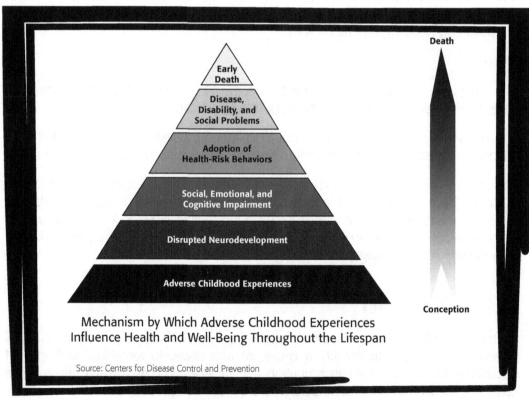

FIGURE 2-1. ACEs PYRAMID

Our hope is that we use the ACEs data and Maslow neuroscience to better understand the impact of stress on the young brain, so we can develop a learning environment that fosters the support and skills to end the negative cycle.

STRESS CAUSES GENE-CHANGING SHIFTS

Young brains exposed to chronic stress, lose the ability to adapt appropriately to future stressful situations, due to changes in gene methylation. Gene methylation is a process where small chemical markers adhere to the genes involved in regulating our stress response, which prevents these genes from doing their jobs. Once these genes are altered, the stress response is on HIGH ALERT for life.

How many times have you experienced that panic-stricken state when your fight/flight/freeze amygdala kicks on? Your heart races, your mouth goes dry, your pupils dilate, and your stomach churns?

Now imagine you were stuck in that panic zone for the rest of your life.

Research shows that the more this stress response is triggered in childhood, the more likely it is to become commonplace throughout adulthood. This is not just an adolescent or hormonal problem. Once this rewiring occurs, the stress of an unexpected bill or someone cutting you off in traffic often leads to explosive reactions throughout life. This also explains why trauma-impacted youth can be violently triggered by seemingly small stressors; their brains simply have been rewired to be overly sensitive to stimuli. This over-reactive response is toxic on many levels and leads to numerous harmful diseases and conditions in the brain and body.

STRESS CHANGES BRAIN STRUCTURE

Distress negatively impacts the brain. In *Research-Based Strategies That Ignite Student Learning*, Dr. Judy Willis shares that TMT (or trimethyltin) is released into the brain during stressful periods, and disrupts healthy cell development, which impairs short-term and/or long-term retention, critical thinking, motivation, and overall cognitive capacity. Dr. Vincent Felitti and his ACEs research shows how the hippocampi (there's one in each hemisphere but like the amygdala/amygdalae they are often referred to in the singular—hippocampus), responsible for spatial awareness, connection, and retention, shrink and lose capacity when stressed, and gray matter, which consists of neurons responsible for retention, seeing, hearing, executive functioning, impulse control, emotions, and speech, also decreases as the result of stress. As a result, large gaps develop in the brain and information is not processed or transferred efficiently. These changes negatively impact one's ability to manage stress and impulses, regulate emotion, and retain knowledge and skills.

THE YOUNG BRAIN IS AN EFFECTIVE GARDENER

Children have an abundance of neurons and the ability to make synaptic connections. Developing brains are hard at work and often referred to as malleable. From birth through adolescence, the brain is constantly "pruning" synaptic connections so that the most vital and important connections are left to drive behavior.

Dr. Margaret McCarthy from Maryland Medical Center explains how ACEs impact this process through non-neuronal brain cells, known as microglia, which are actually part of the immune system. When trauma impacts a child, microglial cells "can get really worked up and crank out neurochemicals that lead to neuroinflammation."

As a result, ACEs dramatically impact a young brain, especially when it lacks the presence of a consistent, loving adult. The impact is massive and can lead to mood disorders, poor executive functioning, and compromised decision-making skills.

CAN WE OVERCOME ACEs?

The answer is a resounding YES. We, as educators, have an important role to play in proactively stopping the adverse effects of ACEs on our Students. Moreover, we have an important role in mitigating the impacts of ACEs in our communities and society.

Following are a few research-based strategies we can employ to help reverse the negative impact of ACEs.

RELATIONSHIPS MATTER, BUT IT'S COMPLICATED

We know this intuitively, yet we sometimes do not explicitly teach how to develop positive relationships with Students or emphasize the tremendous influence they have on Student success. The most recent go-to guide for effect size, John Hattie's *Visible Learning*, noted positive teacher-student relationships have a .72 effect on achievement. The idea, "Kids don't care how much you know, until they know how much you care," is backed up by extensive research.

But have you ever tried to build a positive relationship with a Student and they basically told you to screw off? Relational capacity requires battery charge, and if a Student is drained, he often just can't interact positively. It can be complicated to develop a positive relationship with a traumatized brain because it is in survival mode and it is structurally different. Don't let anyone flippantly tell you, "Just be nice and respectful to him, and he will warm up to you." While it is true that the best "medicine" a student with ACEs can be treated with is to have a consistent, caring adult who provides the support the child needs, what works for non-ACE children may not work for ACEs children. Find what motivates and calms each ACE-impacted brain and make adjustments as necessary. We can provide this differentiated support, and our schools can be a place of healing, instead of a place of continued stress. Addressing the ACEs epidemic is a transformational shift that our school systems must make.

BE CURIOUS, NOT FURIOUS: PERSPECTIVE AND IDENTIFICATION MATTER

A shift in perspective from "What is wrong with this Student?" to "What has this Student suffered?" is sobering. That simple shift in language and mindset for an educator provides an entirely new lens through which to examine and problem-solve.

Schools that are prepared to effectively address the growing ACEs issue have a few things in common:
- Training and resources that produce an understanding of ACEs and/or trauma impacted Students.
- Using this understanding of ACEs and trauma to guide Student behavior policies.
- An awareness of the impact of ACEs on the Students, Staff, and Parents they serve.
- A thorough understanding that school culture and climate must be inclusive, respect diversity, and value protective factors that insulate and support our impacted Students.

UTILIZE TRAUMA-IMPACTED "TRUST-BASED" STRATEGIES

- Provide positive structure and consistency in classroom management.
- Allow Student voice and choice whenever possible.
- Clarify your support role; explain to the Student that you are there to help him be successful, so if there is ever an issue, quickly bring it to your attention in private.
- Establish a "Take a Break" process if the Student is triggered in class. It's an opportunity for him to go to a quiet spot and do something that distracts from the stressor: sketch a picture, work with Play-Doh, or complete a small puzzle.
- Provide a weighted blanket and an area to rest quietly.
- Avoid standing too close or above the child, and yelling; observe personal space, stay eye level or kneel down, and use a calm and low tone of voice.
- Explicitly teach stress management techniques, such as deep breathing, jumping jacks, or squeezing a stress ball.
- Incorporate music, exercise, and art therapy.
- Create a support plan with Staff, so multiple people are aware of the Student's needs and how to help him be successful if you are not available.

TEACH MASLOW AND ACES RESEARCH

Following are three key facts to understand the connection between Maslow and ACEs. For trauma-impacted Students, it is even more important to assess and meet their Maslow needs. Dr. Chris Blodgett—a noted expert in ACEs, their link to long-term mental and physical health issues, and the implications for teaching and learning—provides the following statistics:

1. ACEs are the number-one predictor of Student health, attendance, and behavior.

2. ACEs are the second strongest predictor (Special Education eligibility is number one) of Student academic performance.

3. The relationship between academic achievement and health are more closely tied to exposure to ACEs, than to socio-economic status.

IMPLEMENT SOCIAL-EMOTIONAL LEARNING AND RESTORATIVE PRACTICES

Social-Emotional Learning (SEL) and Restorative Practices have garnered much attention lately. SEL focuses on explicitly teaching executive function and self-regulation skills. In the Edutopia article, "Social and Emotional Learning Research and Review," a meta-analysis of over 200 studies concluded that SEL instruction increases academic performance by 11 percentile points and decreases Students' stress, behavioral, and substance abuse issues.

Restorative Practices allows a misbehaving Student to apologize and receive emotional and behavioral support and redemption opportunities, decreasing the likelihood of recurring misbehavior. When Students are only punitively disciplined, studies such as "The High Cost of High School Dropouts: What the Nation Pays for Inadequate High Schools" have shown they are far more likely to drop out of school, be unemployed, need government assistance, and end up in the prison system.

Julie interviewed Dr. Art Fessler, Superintendent of CCSD 59 in Illinois, who shared how social-emotional learning and restorative practices have positively impacted his school system:

> *"Social-emotional learning takes place when instruction and practice of a specific skill occur. The relationship between meeting needs and teaching skills is clearly demonstrated by the saying, 'Maslow before Bloom.' Students are most likely to learn efficiently when their basic needs have first been met. There are practices that provide support, practices that provide SEL instruction, and practices that do both: Restorative circles and Support circles.*

Restorative circles are part of a continuum of restorative practices that range from less time intensive, informal actions to very time intensive, formal approaches to conflict. According to Costello, Wachtel, & Wachtel (2009), 'restorative' represents a school of thought that, 'decisions are best made and conflicts are best resolved by those most directly involved in them' (p. 7). With student voice and choice taking center stage, this philosophy is not only timely, but best practice. Restorative circles are symbolic gestures. They represent equity of voice, wholeness, and inclusion. Circles are discussions in which participants have equal opportunity to speak about themselves. No one is more important than the next, and all people take ownership and responsibility for themselves. Circles are often facilitated by a 'circle keeper' who poses a question and passes a talking piece. The participants listen to each other, seek to understand each other, and solve problems together. Circles are unlimited in topics and purpose. In District 59, circles have helped promote daily connections and resulted in increased learning and decreased office referrals.

Support circles help students prepare their minds and emotions for learning, and reflect upon their behaviors and beliefs. Circles foster strong relationships, which are the foundation of effective learning environments. District 59 has a high number of students who are experiencing poverty, major societal stressors and fears, and trauma. Those experiences often bring concerns about safety, cause students to see the world in a very different way, and make transitions to and from school increasingly difficult. The act of participating in a Support circle at the beginning and end of the day in our schools, allows students to gain a sense of safety and presence in their learning process, as well as successfully transition in and out of potentially different settings and cultures."

Implementing self-regulating, social-emotional learning and a variety of restorative practices decreases the impact of ACEs on our Students' developing brains and increases Maslow and Bloom success.

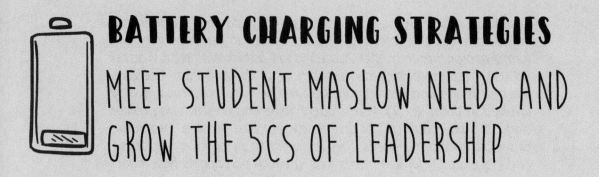

BATTERY CHARGING STRATEGIES
MEET STUDENT MASLOW NEEDS AND GROW THE 5CS OF LEADERSHIP

To be #FULLYCHARGED, consider the following strategies to cultivate competence, confidence, critical thinking, creativity, and compassion in ALL Students.

 ## ASSESS AND MEET MASLOW

This may seem abundantly clear, but it is not. We can strengthen our Students by providing explicit instruction and assessment at EACH grade level in the Maslow areas and raise their level of awareness in these basic needs and the resources to fulfill them, when they are lacking. Student Maslow Assessment is included in Appendix A.

 ## EACH ONE-REACH ONE, STUDENT DRAFT

Every teacher, administrator, and counselor DRAFTS a child who has been identified as needing Maslow support. The Draft process, similar to the NFL Draft, can occur at a Staff or grade-level meeting. The Staff member then devises a plan to reach that child's needs throughout the month and communicates that plan to Staff with updates, via a Google doc or another shared folder. If the Student's needs are met and Draft support is no longer needed, then the Staff member Drafts a different child the next month.

 ## 1X10

Spend one minute a day, 10 days in a row, chatting with a Student. More relationship can be built in a positive one-minute, face-to-face conversation each day, than in a 50-minute class session. Model respectful and positive body language, and thank the Student for the conversation each day; this can be used as a strategy when using the Each One-Reach One Student Draft.

NAP TIME

Arrange for Students who are sleep-deprived to take a nap in another room. This seems counterproductive, but if their home is not safe for sound sleep, we might have to provide it. The young brain requires 9 to 13 hours of sleep every night until the early 20s; it is nearly impossible to learn and regulate emotions when exhausted, as there isn't enough battery charge for attentive concentration.

 # ASSESS ACEs AND PROVIDE SUPPORT

Evaluate Student trauma by asking these questions and create a support plan: Before the age of 18, was the child often emotionally or physically neglected? Was the ACE sudden, expected, or unexpected? How long did it last? Where did the trauma take place, and who was involved? Is the Student still in immediate danger? Does the Student exhibit PTSD symptoms? What is the support system in place? What can still be done to help the Student overcome the trauma? The original ACEs assessment can be found at acestudy.org.

 # SOCIAL-EMOTIONAL LEARNING

Explicitly developing social-emotional skills, or emotional intelligence, is helpful in meeting Maslow needs. Check out casel.org for more information.

Focus on:
- Self-Awareness (identifying emotions, values, and stress triggers)
- Self-Management (managing emotions and behaviors)
- Social Awareness (developing compassion and kindness)
- Relationship Skills (communication, collaboration and conflict resolution)
- Rational Decision-Making (teaching cause and effect, practicing ethical choices)

 # CORRECTIVE CHOICES AND RESTORATIVE BEHAVIORAL INTERVENTIONS AND SUPPORTS

Controlling or disciplining poor behavior after it happens does not equip a Student with the skills to manage his own behavior. To decrease stress (and overall misbehavior) in the classroom, teach self-management strategies, such as squeezing a stress ball or standing at the back counter, instead of sitting, while completing work. Preventative techniques are often more effective than a punishment.

If the Student continues to act out and be a distraction, remember to grow curious, not furious, to determine if the stressor can be eliminated. If the Student needs further correction, instead of automatically assigning detention or kicking him out of class, provide choices. Ask, "Would you like to do 20 jumping jacks right now in the hallway, serve a 15-minute detention after school tomorrow, or write a note of apology explaining what you did wrong and what you will do differently next time?" Allowing the Student a choice in how to manage his stress, and then a choice if correction is necessary, increases his sense of control and ability to self-regulate. Fostering a conversation about the reason for the misbehavior and what to do next time to avoid a consequence helps to develop behavioral awareness. Providing a consequence that can be completed immediately, such as jumping jacks, allows him an opportunity to immediately redeem himself and increases the likelihood that the behavior will improve.

 # SECOND-CHANCE BREAKFAST

Arrange for the cafeteria to provide "Second-Chance Breakfast" during recess times.

 # "BACKSNACKS"

Work with community partners to set up a "BackSnacks" program for those who need food support on non-school days. On Fridays, fill Student backpacks with food for 2+ days of breakfast, snack, and dinner items.

 # ACTION PLANS

When a Student comes from a stressful environment, set up an actionable plan for transitions and community support before weekends and long breaks. Make sure the Student (and Parent/s) know whom to contact for food, shelter, and other Maslow needs, when school is not in session.

 # "IT'S COOL TO BE CONNECTED" CAMPAIGN

Start a campaign to get each Student involved in at least one school club, sport or extracurricular activity, and focus on promoting positive relationships throughout their involvement. Consider Ping-Pong, board game, exercise, art, and/or community service clubs, and build community by "branding" the club with a logo, a slogan, and shirts, bracelets, and so forth.

"NEURO NUGGETS"

Consider spending just one minute each day teaching one brain or body healthy habit, such as the importance of adequate sleep, hydration, exercise, stress management, and the like. We refer to these as Neuro Nuggets, which are tips for keeping our brains healthy and strong. Some schools incorporate this idea into their morning announcements or into their health and physical education classes. When we know better, we do better, and Students benefit from learning about making good choices regarding their health, early on and often.

POSITIVE LEADERSHIP MINDSETS

Start class with a positive affirmation. The mind is very powerful. Henry Ford said, "Whether you think you can or you think you can't, you're right." Consider this 5C Leadership statement: "I am a competent, confident, compassionate, and creative critical thinker. I will be successful, if I do not give up! If I get stuck, I can ask for help. I will help others so they can be successful, too. My teacher cares about me and wants me to be successful, so I will ask for help when I need it."

MENTORING MATTERS

Place younger Students who need to feel acceptance with older "Mentor" Students who naturally are friendly and welcoming. Have them meet regularly for snacks, tutoring, enrichment, and games.

FLEXIBLE SEATING

Flexible seating learning environments provide a warm welcome for Students. The ability to choose a learning space is empowering for many and creates a sense of belonging. Keep it simple: have an area for desks, another for carpet sitting, and an area for standing.

VOICE AND CHOICE

Provide choices in assignments, assessments, engagement, and collaboration (Genius Hour, PBL, Maker Spaces, etc.), and help Students discover their strengths and passions. Tailor their assignments and group work around the areas in which they are strong.

INSIDE OUT FAMILY MOVIE NIGHT

Host an evening pajama party and show the *Inside Out* cartoon. It is an excellent portrayal of the five emotions and how they influence Student success. Dr. Lori Desautels developed a FREE curriculum to accompany the movie to share with Students, Parents and Staff. It's available in her blog series on Edutopia, titled: "How Emotions Affect Learning, Behaviors, and Relationships."

 ## GROWTH MINDSET AND RETAKES

Teach a growth mindset as discussed in Carol Dweck's book *Mindset*, and allow retakes often to celebrate the learning that comes from making mistakes. Focus on Student academic and behavior improvement, not immediate perfection.

 ## WHAT INTERESTS YOU?

Encourage Students to research their interests; www.thrively.com is a free website where they can self-assess and identify their passions and strengths.

 ## YOU CAN ALWAYS SIT WITH US

Provide a safe lunchtime connection place for Students who aren't feeling very connected. Staff it with older, friendly Students or Staff, and make it available every day for reading, puzzles, drawing and such, so no one ever sits alone.

 ## COLOR BLIND OR COLOR BRAVE?

Cultivate Color Braveness instead of Color Blindness:
- Celebrate diversity and acknowledge language, culture, and race as strengths.
- Build relationships with your Students and connect with ALL families.
- Ask questions about differences and show appreciation.
- Engage in honest conversations about diversity on the campus with colleagues and administrators.
- Get comfortable with being uncomfortable and not having all the answers.

- Learn about diversity and culturally responsive teaching.
- Provide culturally relevant Student books.

To learn more, view Rosa's blog with more resources, in Appendix C.

 # FOUR BEFORE THE DOOR

Do these four things each day with each Student before they exit the door: make eye contact, smile, greet by name, provide one compliment or ask Student about one thing they are involved in (art, athletics, music, etc.) to foster positive connection. Logistically, for Staff who have hundreds of Students, do these four each week before Students exit class on Friday.

 # POSITIVE LUNCH BUNCH

Each week, identify four to five Students with Maslow needs and invite them to have lunch with a beloved Staff member. It's great when it is the Principal, but it is also wonderful when it is a Custodian, Librarian, Teacher, or such. When Students leave, provide a handwritten note of encouragement and a special treat, such as a pack of colored pencils or a snack.

 # POSITIVE CALLS, TEXTS, AND VISITS

Make weekly positive phone calls, emails, or home visits, even if it seems there isn't anything to praise. Students who come from stressful homes sometimes just need praise—for anything. Sharing a compliment with a family member can help the family to recognize the positives about the Student also, creating even more positives. Make the goal of *at least* four positive contacts per week; those Students who struggle academically or behaviorally need them the most.

#FULLYCHARGED WRAP-UP

To increase social-emotional ecstasy in the young brain and maximize our energy and resources, here are a few questions and final thoughts to guide your steps in meeting Student Maslow needs:

- How will you assess your Students' Maslow needs?
- What resources will you provide to meet those needs?
- How can your Staff collaboratively meet the needs and share updates?

Students bring their rechargeable brains through our school doors every day; some arrive #FULLYCHARGED, and some are dragging and nearly depleted.

Just like Brian in Julie's class, he showed up the day after being absent with a nearly drained battery, so drained in fact that he was suicidal. When she made it a point to let him know he was missed, that was all this troubled eighth-grader needed to hear to charge his battery a bit, and it literally saved his life.

Though it didn't immediately fix his Bloom struggles, Julie was helpful in a way that she wasn't even aware, just by checking in with him every day and letting him know that he was missed after being absent. Sometimes what our Students need to recharge their battery is so simple, yet so profound.

Many of our Students are like Brian, Tyrone, or Jenny, forced to accept responsibility for circumstances completely out of their control, and that is a heavy burden to bear. All the while, they hope someone will notice and fill the void, or better yet, keep them safe.

Stress is not a respecter of socio-economic status. Though the stressors may be different, Students at all points on the socio-economic spectrum are impacted by stress. Our diverse population of Students is fighting a variety of short- and long-term stressors on multiple levels of severity. It is up to us, as educators, to show empathy and meet Students where they are AND help decrease their stress. To increase our system's effectiveness, we must not only identify the Maslow needs of our Students, but be intentional in filling the necessary void before pressing them to expend cognitive energy on academic goals.

Once we identify Student need, we can systematically design an environment that fosters social-emotional ecstasy.

Why?

Because it strengthens, encourages, and cares for Students in a way that recharges their batteries so they can in turn, strengthen, encourage, and care for others.

Isn't that the purpose of education?

"Educating the mind without educating the heart is no education at all."

—Aristotle

#FULLYCHARGED
CHAPTER 2: BOOK STUDY/ TWITTER CHAT QUESTIONS

1. Describe a Student you know whose Maslow needs are not being met. How does this influence his/her academic success?

2. How does your school system identify and support Student Maslow needs?

3. What are two neuroscience principles from this chapter that will most influence how you interact with Students?

4. Have you, or anyone close to you, suffered multiple ACEs? If so, what has the long-term impact been?

5. Identify three ideas that resonate with you from this chapter. How will you share those ideas with your Students/Parents/Staff?

Please visit effectiveteachingpd.com or mbsimplesolution.com to watch the #FULLYCHARGED Author Chat about this chapter and participate in our 21 Day Challenge.

CHAPTER 3
Meeting Parent Maslow Needs

"Raising kids is a walk in the park: Jurassic Park."

"I always used to wonder why people couldn't control their kids in public, and then I had my own."

"I'm amazed by the parents who are teaching their children how to play the violin and speak multiple languages, while I'm over here just trying to get mine to stop licking the counter."

"Once upon a time I was a perfect parent, AND then I had children. The End."

"Parent: NO.

Child: I feel that you are not completely committed to that NO, so I'm going to ask you 454 more times to test your commitment."

"The hardest part of parenting is realizing that THIS IS MY CIRCUS and these ARE MY MONKEYS."

"Parenting is the definition of HARD."

*   *   *   *   *

> *"As educators, we often focus on Student needs, as we should, but to get to the root of Student struggles, we should also consider and address Parent needs.*
>
> —Julie Adams

I (Julie) was teaching at a large middle school in northern California and was out on dropoff circle duty on a chilly, winter morning.

A beat-up car with a rattling muffler pulled up to drop off a Student. The door opened, and out stepped a seventh-grade boy. From inside the car, I heard his mom scream at the top of her lungs, "AND ANOTHER THING YOU ALWAYS F****** DO WRONG IS _____! I CAN'T TAKE IT ANYMORE!"

He turned around and quietly said, "I know, Mama. I'm sorry..." And with slouched shoulders, he slowly walked toward class as she raced out of the dropoff zone.

I shuddered and wondered if he would be able to concentrate on learning math equations and persuasive writing techniques that day after such an early stressful interaction with his Parent.

That was my second year of teaching and maybe the first time it clearly occurred to me that some of our Students arrive at school with a drained battery, not having enough cognitive energy to devote to academics, after struggling to survive their home environment.

Later that day during my prep period, I walked through the office, and who did I see sitting outside the principal's door? Yep, that same kid.

I stopped and introduced myself.

"Hey there, how's it going? My name is Mrs. Adams, and I teach English and U.S. History. What's your name?"

No response.

"Okay, well if you ever need anything, I'm in room 204, just down the hallway. I'm there from dawn until dusk on most days, so just stop on by."

As I turned to walk away, he mumbled, "Justin."

I turned toward him, "What's that? Did you say your name is Justin? It's nice to meet you, Justin. Can I help you with anything?"

"Got anything to eat?"

"Yes, don't go anywhere. I'll be right back."

"Lady, I'm not going anywhere."

I hurried to the cafeteria and asked our amazing cafeteria Super Woman if she had any extra items she could put on my tab so I could feed a hungry Student. She handed me a muffin, banana, and a milk and a BIG smile.

Oh, how I love all the people in a school system who LOVE kids!

"Hey, Justin, how about these?"

He gobbled them up. I asked him a few more questions, but he made it clear that he was done with me. I walked away continuing to think about him.

I later found out that Justin had been in our K-8 school system for several years, failed nearly all his classes and been in and out of academic intervention without success. He lived in low-income housing, and he was a lone wolf who was NOT signed up for our Free and Reduced Breakfast and Lunch Program because his mom had never returned the paperwork. Most attention he received throughout the day was disciplinary.

I was curious as to what was going on in his Mama's life that would cause her to be so frustrated and angry.

As educators, we often focus on Student needs, as we should, but to get to the root of Student struggles, we should consider and address Parent needs also.

Remember the earlier quote, "If you plant a seed and it does not flourish, you do not blame the seed." It's often not the seed, but the environment, that needs to be adjusted.

Meeting Parent Maslow needs are important to a successful leadership culture because they are often the first and last points of daily contact for Students and a fundamental part of their battery charge and environment.

So to effectively meet a struggling Student's needs, we should also ask, "What are the stressors in the Parents' life, AND how can we help?"

*　　*　　*　　*　　*

"In retrospect, I wish the teachers who doubted my Parents had taken the time to meet them where they were."

—Rosa Isiah

I (Rosa) grew up in poverty with Parents who struggled in getting their Maslow needs met. They worked extremely hard to just "get by," and, therefore, were always in survival mode. They were non-English speaking immigrants, who wanted a better opportunity for their children, but struggled to navigate a new system. They lacked education and the social capital to connect with resources. They worried about paying the light bill and clothing and feeding their children.

Our home life was in a constant state of stress. THEY were in a constant state of stress.

I remember dreading big school events as a child. I knew my Parents wouldn't be able to attend. At the time I didn't understand how difficult it would be for my Parents to take time off work for Parent conferences or celebrations. If they missed a day of work, they gave up a day's pay, and we simply could not afford it.

For many working Parents, especially undocumented families, a missed day may often lead to loss of employment. As an elementary Student, I also remember teachers making statements about my Parents: "She's bright, but doesn't have home support" or "Her parents don't care, they never attend conferences or functions."

The statements were not only hurtful, but they were completely inaccurate. My Parents loved me and were proud of my hard work. They couldn't believe how quickly I had become a fluent English speaker and writer. They wanted me to grow up and to do better than they ever dreamt for themselves. They bragged every chance they had about my successes.

My Parents' physiological and safety needs were never met, resulting in those same fears for myself and my siblings. I wasn't alone in this experience. There were MANY families in my community who were also in survival mode and needed support for themselves and their children. In retrospect, I wish the teachers who doubted my Parents had taken the time to meet them where they were.

When our schools take a "whole family" approach to meeting Parent needs and engaging them in the learning process, our Students, Parents, and Staff win!

I often use my own experiences to guide and strengthen my approach to Parent engagement as a teacher and a school administrator. We must actively seek to meet both Maslow and Bloom, every day, for every Student, and every Family.

"Is it any surprise that some Parents have negative perceptions about school, when their own experience was negative and nearly every interaction with their child's school has also been negative?"

PJ Caposey

I (PJ) was in my early 30s and a Principal at the time. It was mid-year, and I was anxious for the busy week to be over. I was headed out of town on a well-needed weekend away with friends. Really, it is a little embarrassing how excited I was for this getaway.

The plan was for my friend, Tim, to meet me at the school around 3, and once the school cleared of all the Students, we would head out for the weekend. I was dropped off at work that morning; my luggage sat in the corner of my Principal's office, staring at me as the day inched along.

At 1:30, I was finishing up my weekly report to my Superintendent when a call for me rang out over the radio. A small fracas had broken out in the shop classroom. Within a few minutes, order was restored, and I spent the rest of my afternoon attempting to contact Parents and complete the incident's paperwork.

All in all, it was a typical day in the life of a school administrator.

About 2:30, I looked up and remembered that my friend would soon be in the office. I picked up my phone intending to text him I would be a little delayed, when in walked a Parent I had been trying to contact about the shop class incident.

The Parent meeting was very positive and, as it ended, I looked into the main office area and saw my buddy waiting for me. I invited him in and apologized for the delay. He said it was no problem and sat down while I finished up the report.

After a few minutes, I looked up to see him visibly dismayed. I shot off some snarky comment about him being put off having to wait an extra 15 minutes for me. He looked at me, shook his head, and said, "Nah, forget it. You would never understand."

I pressed and finally he leaned forward and nervously confided, "I know this is crazy, but I am just really uncomfortable being in the Principal's office." I laughed and said, "Come on, really? I have known you since we were 19."

He explained to me how he would often get in trouble at school, particularly elementary school. He did not have a single fond, or even neutral, memory of stepping foot in the Principal's office. He acknowledged that it was strange that he felt that way given his age and our positive relationship, but he just could not shake that negative feeling, or his anxiety.

Wow! Tim was now in his mid-30s, involved in the community, coached youth sports, and served on various boards and committees. He was successful and doing extremely well financially, with ownership rights to several small businesses. He was also very involved with his own kids' schooling.

In spite of all this, he was visibly disturbed sitting in the Principal's office. Moreover, as I asked questions about his experiences, they could easily be categorized as underwhelming. A few detentions, a call or two to a Parent that led to some harsh consequences, and one incident that led to strong language from the Principal and a referral. For many people reading this, his experience did not sound unlike many of ours, just some ordinary elementary mischief.

But this anxiety had stuck with him. This impacted him. This forever changed his associations about school and the Principal's office.

In that one interaction, I learned more about myself and presuppositions about working with Parents than I had learned in any class, any book, or in all my years of experience combined. What I learned: not everyone remembers school as this amazing place where you found your identity and destiny, made friends, and created a lifetime of warm and fuzzy memories.

I could now empathize with the discomfort some of the Parents who entered my office must have felt in previous interactions.

Imagine if my friend had been racially discriminated against or experienced some other type of injustice? What if the consequence received in the office led to physical abuse at home or perhaps a consequence had altered someone's life through an expulsion, removal from a team, or a lost opportunity?

This could lead to well-intentioned, caring adults perceiving school as a very scary and unsafe place to be. This perception may not be immediately visible, and it has nothing to do with socioeconomic status, race, religion, creed, OR how his child is performing.

This negative perception had to do exclusively with his own experience as a Student, which in all likelihood, had nothing to do with the current adults in the school system.

Think about how this manifests differently when issues are not behavioral, but academic. Some Parents struggle with academic efficacy. This frustration, or even embarrassment, can manifest in a number of negative ways and is rooted in a lack of competence and confidence around their own academic struggles.

Imagine meeting with a concerned Parent. You're sitting behind your big desk, in your business suit, with your educational merits hanging behind you, and that Parent has suffered with literacy or numeracy and just being on a school campus triggers their flight/flight/freeze response?

That meeting may be set for failure before it even begins.

As Rosa illustrated in her narrative above, do schools with bilingual Students consider how stressful it can be for Parents who, due to language barriers, cannot interact with us in order to support their children?

As a Parent who currently struggles to not be a "helicopter," I know how necessary it is to engage in my children's education and provide support when necessary. I cannot even fathom what it would be like to not be able to speak the same language as the educators instructing my child while also being unfamiliar with the standards, curricula, and strategies that educators use.

Considering these perspectives fundamentally changes the game when it comes to creating a positive culture in your school community and leveraging your Parents as collaborative partners in the learning process. It amplifies the challenge of creating a school environment that is welcoming and successful in developing human and leadership capacity. Sometimes our gestures will work for those who have a blank slate or positive impression of school, but it may not work for everyone.

It would not work for my friend. Our challenge is to go beyond creating a welcoming environment and working to proactively engage and sometimes recreate the image of what school is for many of our Parents.

Simply put, we have to take care of our Parents. We cannot expect them to be our "partner" in educating their Students when they have had no positive experiences in a school setting.

Rocket Science Research

Though we started this chapter with some jokes about parenting, the task is no laughing matter.

There are three reasons that make it worthwhile for our school systems to meet Parent Maslow needs.

First, Parenting is hard. It is a skill, and not all have it.

Second, in order for Parents (or Caregivers serving as Parents) to effectively meet their Student's needs, their own needs must be met to have enough battery charge for positive Parenting. Just as the flight attendant on a plane states, "If we experience a sudden loss of cabin pressure, please secure your own oxygen mask first, before assisting your child," we should practice self-care to have enough capacity to care for others.

Third, if we cultivate competence, confidence, compassion, creativity, and critical thinking in Parents, then they are more likely to have positive associations toward our school system and be more willing to partner with us to grow capacity in our Students. Therefore, we maximize our system's efficiency when we collaborate with Parents to establish the environment conducive to fostering the 5 Cs of Leadership.

Now, more than ever, Parents need sleep, security, social acceptance, and confidence in order to reach their full creative and critical thinking potential. When these basic needs are not met, there is an increase in mental and physical health problems.

According to the World Health Organization's "Depression Fact Sheet 2017," depression is a serious and common mental disorder, affecting more than 300 million people worldwide, and it is the leading cause of disability. Though treatment can be effective, less than half of those suffering seek it.

Harvard psychiatrist Dr. William Beardslee is noted for his extensive study and involvement in the report: "Untreated, Unrecognized Parental Depression Can Lead to Negative Consequences for Kids." He provides insight into acknowledging that a Parent's mental health dramatically impacts the care a child receives. This is not a controversial statement. It's a fact.

Parental mental health has long-term influence on our Students' health, ranging from decreased school performance, increased emergency room visits, noted relationship issues inside and outside the home, and an increase in adolescent anxiety and depression.

ACEs Parents

In the previous chapter, we discussed Adverse Childhood Experiences and how they negatively impact Students' abilities and success. Schools are becoming more skillful at responding to Students' social-emotional needs, but we must continue to improve, lest we forget that our current ACE-impacted Students will someday be the Parents of our future Students.

Many of our current Parents also suffered ACEs; as a result, they often operate in the fight/flight/freeze mode and can struggle with post traumatic stress and attachment disorders. This cycle is perpetuating and unhealthy for our society.

> "It is easier to build strong children than to repair broken men."
>
> —Frederick Douglass

We are not naive in thinking that meeting Parent needs is easy. In some respect, as Frederick Douglass noted, it may be easier to help our struggling Students than it is to strengthen their Parents. However, with so much at stake, it should be one of our goals as educators.

Where can we start?

PARENT TRAINING IS BENEFICIAL

Several studies have shown that providing explicit Parent Effectiveness Training (PET) sessions focused on interpersonal skills, emotional intelligence, and problem solving strategies does positively impact the relationships within a family. Parenttraining.com is a free resource packed with research and ideas for parenting trainings.

Following is a clip from their site sharing the benefits of teaching parenting skills:

> *"Controlled studies have demonstrated positive attitudinal changes in parents taking PET (Schultz, 1981; Schultz, Nystul & Law, 1980). Schultz (1981) showed that PET had positive effects on specific family members, including mothers, fathers and children. Fathers were likely to become less authoritarian, mothers more positive about child-rearing, and children increased their positive relationships with both parents.*
>
> *Positive attitudinal change was demonstrated in parents after PET by Schultz, Nystul and Law, (1980) and matching behavioural changes were shown by Schultz and Nystul (1980). Schultz and Kahn (1982) reported that following PET, mothers demonstrated improved microskills with their young children in short-term interactions. These included appreciative comments, touching, actively seeking the child's opinion and an ability to manage disagreement.*
>
> *Rob and Norfor (1980) who compared the outcomes of PET participants with population norms on the same measures, found that parents*

who had completed PET showed greater confidence in their ability as parents, were more aware of the influence of the environment on their children and had a more trusting relationship with them...

In another study (Wood & Davidson, 1993) it was shown that parents and adolescent children taking PET and YET (Youth Effectiveness Training) respectively, acquired the ability to make behavioural changes in their interactions, with both groups demonstrating significant improvement in conflict resolution skills compared with controls. Compared with the control group, the PET parents improved significantly in Assertiveness and Conflict Resolution, with a trend for improvement in Active Listening." (http://www.parenttraining.com.au/resources/research/)

HELPING PARENTS MANAGE STRESS

Dr. Kristen Race, author of *Mindful Parenting*, explains how it benefits us to tackle Parent stress because stressed Parents often produce stressed children. Generation X, those born between 1965 and 1985ish, are all grown up. In 2010, the American Psychological Association's "Stress in America" study named them "The Most Stressed Generation in America" according to how they choose to manage their stress compared to other generations. According to the study, many have poor eating habits, low exercise levels, and suffer from chronic sleep deprivation, due to excessive screen time. A whopping 56 percent of them reported feeling extremely irritable, or even angry, most of the time. In 2013, their children, or Generation Z, assumed this title.

Stress is debilitating and also contagious, so it's no coincidence that stressed Generation X, gave birth to the even more stressed Generation Z. We have mirror neurons in our brains which promote a strong desire to mimic others' behavior, even stressful behavior. That is why we want to yawn, or cry, when we see someone else do it.

Stress drains our battery charge and our abilities to show compassion and empathy. Parents who lack these characteristics, can have behavior that is detrimental to our Students.

According to Dr. Karyl McBride, the author of *Will I Ever Be Good Enough?*:

"Lack of empathy is a trademark of narcissistic parents. Empathizing with your children is feeling what they are feeling and acknowledging those feelings. It is the art of compassion and sensitivity, as well as the ability to give moral support in whatever they are experiencing, that strengthens a child. You do not have to agree with them, but you are there for them. You put aside your own feelings and thoughts for the moment and tune in to their emotional needs to attempt to understand where they are coming from and why."

This insight is meaningful because ACEs Parents often behave in a narcissistic manner unintentionally. Knowing this, emphasizes the importance of meeting Parent Maslow needs, to increase their capacity for compassion in order to strengthen their children.

LEGISLATING AND MANDATING PARENT SUPPORT

Research has concluded that Parents are indeed one of the most influential factors for Student success, with some states now even legislating how schools interact and engage Parents in the learning process.

For example, California educates over 6 million children and young adults each year, and is home to over 10,000 schools. This is no simple feat.

Legislators and educators often look to research for guidance. Recently, a meta-analysis was released by EdSource, *The Power of Parents*, that is guiding legislation and policy in California, and many states are now following their lead:

> *"The dramatic reform of California's school funding system, currently being implemented in schools across the state, calls for involving parents in their children's schools in two important ways:*
>
> * *Schools must get input from parents as to how additional state funds intended for low-income students, English learners and foster children are spent.*
> * *Parent involvement is one of eight 'priority areas' identified by the state, and schools will be assessed as to how successful they are in working with parents.*
>
> *EdSource, in collaboration with New America Media, has conducted a review of the voluminous research on the value and impact of parent engagement on their children's performance and the schools they attend, especially as it relates to the California experience.*
>
> *Much of the research on parent involvement is written for an academic or policy audience, often in very abstract terms. But these are some of the principal conclusions that can be drawn from the examination of much of the research:*
>
> * *Parent involvement at home and at school has a measurable impact on student performance in school, and is particularly important for English learners and students from low-income families.*
> * *Parent involvement is related to improved student behavior in school and better attitudes about school work generally.*
> * *Improved communication between teachers and parents increases student engagement as measured by homework completion rates, on-task behavior and class participation.*

- *At-risk behaviors such as alcohol use, violence and other anti-social behaviors decrease as parent involvement increases."
(https://edsource.org/wp-content/publications/Power-of-Parents-Feb-2014.pdf)*

California's Education Code Section 11504, specifically requires that school districts establish a "parent involvement program for each school" and provides descriptions as to what the program should include.

The National School Boards Association and the National PTA uses the 6-part framework, "Schools, Family, and Community Partnerships," as an outline for school systems to encourage, strengthen, and care for our Caregivers.

The framework focuses on school-parent partnership in these areas:
- Help with parenting
- Two-way communication
- Volunteering
- Learning at home
- Decision-making
- Collaboration

This framework also serves as the foundation for "California's Family Engagement Network" which guides schools in developing and/or expanding school to home support, to meet Student and Parent needs to increase achievement.

As previously mentioned, there are many reasons why it can be difficult to reach out to and strengthen our Parent base; however, the value (and mandates) override the cost.

HOW DO YOU RATE?

With anxiety and depression at an all-time high, it is clear that many have needs that are unmet. Answer these questions first for yourself AND then for your closest friends, to find out how well your basic needs are being met (see survey format in Appendix B).

- Physiological
  - ✓ Are you in healthy physical condition?
  - ✓ Can you (physically) do everything you want to do?
  - ✓ Have you made choices that promote a long and healthy life (regularly exercise, eat healthy, manage stress, limit screen time, etc.)?

- Safety
  - ✓ Are you financially secure?
  - ✓ Do you feel financially prepared for retirement or a health emergency?
  - ✓ Do you feel safe and secure at home, work, and in your community?

- Love and Belonging
  - ✓ Are you engaged in meaningful, personal relationships?
  - ✓ Do you have positive relationships with your family?
  - ✓ Do you have friends to connect with and feel emotionally connected to?

- Esteem
  - ✓ Do you respect yourself and feel respected by others?
  - ✓ Do you find intrinsic value in doing things for others that do not result in prestige or financial gain?

- Self-Actualization
  - ✓ Do you have a strong grip on who you are and are capable of being?
  - ✓ Have you become your best self?
  - ✓ Are you a Battery Drainer or Charger?

When Adult Maslow Needs are broken down to this level, it is pretty clear that many are not getting all of their needs met. This is intended to be eye-opening because if the needs of our Students' Caregivers are not being met, how can they possibly meet the needs of others?

WHAT CAN HAPPEN WHEN WE MEET STUDENT AND PARENT NEEDS?

What happened to Justin, the Student I (Julie) witnessed being dropped off by the enraged mother?

Though he made it clear that he did not want further contact with me at that time (which sometimes happens, and it hurts but it's usually not personal, nor is it the end of our responsibility), I was able to connect Justin with two people on campus that he did respond to well.

He clicked with a male teacher, Mr. Johnson, who also coached track and provided lunchtime homework help, so he got the help he needed, started completing his assignments, joined the track team, and passed his classes.

He also connected with one of our fantastic counselors, so he received weekly social-emotional counseling.

Their phone was disconnected, so I went to their apartment, located in the low-income housing section of our school zone. I knocked on the door with a hot coffee and a footlong turkey sandwich in my hands for his mama, because my mama taught me to never show up empty-handed.

She reluctantly invited me in after I introduced myself, blurted out that I had never made a home visit before, and then asked, "Is there anything I can do to help your son be more successful at school?"

It is amazing what a stranger will tell you when you ask a question and then wait for a response.

As she gobbled up the sandwich, she explained that she was not living the life she dreamed, but she felt she had nowhere to turn. She was an only child and both her parents were deceased. She had gotten pregnant with Justin after a one night stand with a stranger, and his father was not in the picture.

After a series of poor choices and unfortunate events, she and her teen son were now barely treading water.

I asked her to come to the school the next day to sign Justin up for the free and reduced breakfast and lunch program and the low-income student insurance plan which would provide Justin with a free medical, dental, and eye exam. She complained that she had arthritis in her hands which made it difficult to fill out paperwork, so I promised to meet her in the office and help her with it.

We talked for a few minutes more, and I learned a great deal about them. I wanted to help.

The next morning, I met her in the school office to complete the paperwork.

A few weeks later, I knocked on her door again. She was rushing out to her job as an evening custodian at a local office building. This time she smiled when she saw me and she told me that Justin had already seen the eye doctor, and he needed glasses! He had 20/500 vision! She cried as she recounted how he often complained about his head hurting and how he couldn't understand his school work and that's why she was yelling at him at dropoff that one morning; she thought he was just being lazy!

She sobbed as she explained how bad she felt that his struggles were in large part due to her parenting failures. She had blamed him for being negative and incompetent, but in reality, he really needed food, glasses, and counseling.

I again handed her a footlong sandwich and an extra for him, along with a few gifts. I had purchased a backpack for Justin in his favorite color, dark blue, along with some school supplies, and a thick Seattle Seahawks sweatshirt, also his favorite.

I asked her if she would give the gifts to Justin and say they were from her, not me. She agreed and shared that she had always wanted to get him those things, but could never afford it.

Again she cried.

"Is there anything else I can help you with?" I asked. She then admitted she didn't have arthritis, but needed help with her reading skills because she couldn't understand the paperwork that often came home from the school; that was why she had never completed the Free and Reduced Meal information.

Then she confided that she had been molested when she was younger, and she asked if I knew anyone who could provide counseling to her.

Her admissions made me cry. Justin's mama was an illiterate, ACEs Parent, and she needed help.

For the next several months, Justin was dropped off every morning sporting his Seahawks sweatshirt and backpack. He blossomed as he received the Maslow and Bloom support he needed.

His mama received extensive tutoring and counseling and went on to help others by working in women's shelters and victim advocacy. Justin recently graduated from law school, #FULLYCHARGED with Honors, wearing Seahawk socks.

I'm fairly certain that he will change the world for the better, and his mama will be right there by his side.

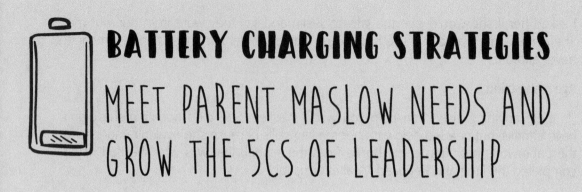

BATTERY CHARGING STRATEGIES
MEET PARENT MASLOW NEEDS AND GROW THE 5CS OF LEADERSHIP

To be #FULLYCHARGED, consider the following strategies to cultivate competence, confidence, compassion, and creative, critical thinking in Parents.

 ## CREATE POSITIVE SOCIAL-EMOTIONAL EXPERIENCES WITHIN THE SCHOOL

Great educators understand that while Parents want a great education for their Student, not everyone has the resources to help make the schooling experience even more successful.

By offering Parent workshops, support groups, and other forms of outreach, the Students will reap multiple benefits. These activities can be as simple as getting lists of sight words into the hands of primary grades Parents, leveraging social media and other software platforms to expand communication and learning opportunities, or as complex as providing multi-session workshops with outside presenters on how to best establish routines, positive communication, and boundaries for a middle schooler.

Such actions have multiple positive benefits for schools and educators:
- Ultimately, the time spent working with current and future Parents will benefit our Students.
- The more positive contact we have, the greater the opportunity for Parents to gain a greater level of comfort interacting with the school. This comfort, coupled with the sentiment that the school has provided them with a truly useful skill, undoubtedly will help build productive community relationships.

CREATE A MASLOW-RICH ENVIRONMENT FOR ALL

It is important for schools to understand it is beneficial to bridge the gaps with those who did not enjoy their school experience, prior to the time those people have school-aged children. A school can provide services that are needed in the community and transform the school into a safe and fun place for those who once had a less-than-ideal experience.

To increase Parent participation, ease the issues many face in trying to attend by providing FREE food, childcare, and homework help to young children. Increase motivation by offering door prizes, upbeat music, and Parent participation points that can be redeemed later, such as for free entrance into a school event or for spirit clothing.

Tap into the expertise in your community to provide support and services for your families. Many experts in finance, health, law enforcement, tech, counseling, culinary, fitness, business, and such are thrilled to lend a hand and share their services in our school communities.

Educators who actively invite Parents (and community members) into the school, for both school and non-school related activities, and ensure they have a positive experience, are FAR more likely to positively influence their associations about school and develop the trust and positive relationships that foster partnership between the home and school.

SPEED GEEKING

Provide several 15-minute sessions during a 90-minute evening event to Parents about different topics they can rotate through, instead of providing over an hour on a single topic. Provide several topics to choose from, or survey Parents about their interest in a variety of topics and offer them accordingly. Then after Speed Geeking Night, survey Parents to find out which topics they want more in-depth knowledge about and plan future sessions accordingly. It can be overwhelming to sit through a lengthy session about digital literacy or social-emotional learning. Many benefit more by briefly dipping their toes into a few topics and walking away with one or two ideas, rather than being bombarded with too much about a single topic too soon, leaving them overwhelmed and intimidated.

PARENT UNIVERSITY

Based on survey responses, offer in-depth multi-session evenings on complex topics such as athletic recruiting, the college application process, and completing the Federal Application for Student Aid (FAFSA). Record the sessions, and make them available on the school website and Facebook page to increase Parent reachability.

 # ASSESS PARENT MASLOW NEEDS, AND PROVIDE RESOURCES FOR SUCCESS

Have Parents take our Adult Maslow Assessment (Appendix B) and then provide insight and resources into how to get their needs met if they are lacking. Many districts offer food, clothing, school supplies, and counseling services to families of our Students. Many are not aware of all that is available to them.

 # ASSESS PARENT ACEs, AND PROVIDE SUPPORT FOR SUCCESS

Many are ACEs Parents, yet do not have any experience as to what that means and how to overcome it. Have an expert provide mini-sessions on the topic and how to address it to increase battery charge and success. Following are a few ideas to share: the link between trauma and addiction, untreated trauma is linked to the development of a variety of mental and physical health issues, untreated trauma can impact our compassion which negatively affects our children, and one can have had a happy childhood but still have experienced ACEs.

 # #FULLYCHARGED NIGHT—THE POWER OF POSITIVITY

Research has shown that positivity increases our cognitive capacity. Host a #FULLYCHARGED Positivity Power Night, and provide short Speed Geeking sessions on all things POSITIVE that increase our battery charge such as: Positive Parenting ideas (control emotional outbursts, share one or two positives per night with family, have 10 minutes of uninterrupted positive and open-ended conversation with Student on most days, provide at least one positive comment to child each day), Positive Stress Relievers (exercise, laughter, upbeat music, acts of kindness), Positive Feedback strategies, Positive Eating Habits, Positive Homework Help Ideas, Positive Reading Habits, and so forth.

LUNCHTIME STUDENT-PARENT MAKERSPACE LABS

One or two days per month, offer a 30-minute small group Makerspace activity for a few Students and their Parents, such as constructing a house out of mini-marshmallows and toothpicks, and provide lunch. Students can be nominated or chosen by lottery. If a Parent can't attend, then the Student can choose a Staff member to participate. These quick, collaborative activities are great for building relationship and enhancing critical thinking skills, while also teaching adults how simple it is to play and chat with youth.

PARENTING PALS SUPPORT GROUP

With anxiety and depression being diagnosed at alarming rates, consider providing consistent parenting support groups. It can be helpful to have a safe forum to ask questions, share problems, hear solutions, and celebrate successes that vary in topic from potty training, to homework conflicts, to establishing routines and boundaries in the home. Group discussions also develop camaraderie and let Parents know that they are not the only ones struggling with an issue. They are also a great way for Parents to learn more about other kids in their child's age range and set up playdates to help them develop relationships, too.

THE POWER OF CONNECTION

Provide Family Art, Math Mania, Magical Movie, and Game Nights. Marketing matters. Come up with catchy titles for the nights and fun themes. After, send home a few questions and activity suggestions with families that can be discussed later at home to continue the connection and critical thinking that occurred throughout the event.

VIRTUAL BOOK CLUB

Book Clubs are popular for a reason: they build community. Host an in-person or virtual Facebook or Google Hangout Parent Book Club every semester focused on a different hot topic book such as *Brain Rules* by John Medina, *The Teenage Brain* by Frances Jensen, *Mindset* by Carol Dweck, or *The Happiness Advantage* by Shawn Achor. Focus on just one or two chapters every few weeks, establish a time on social media when the book will be discussed and invite EVERYONE (including Staff), to participate. Each book is reader friendly and packed with stories and strategies to increase success in ourselves and the children we are raising.

MENTORING MATTERS

Some need support in mentoring and guiding their children. Maybe it's a single mom desiring male mentoring for her young sons, or a grandparent needing assistance in raising grandchildren, after decades of not having children in the home. Whatever the case, establishing a Male/Female mentoring program and calling on volunteers from the community to serve (after they have received training) in mentoring roles is a powerful way to meet these needs. The Boys and Girls Clubs of America provide support and guidelines in how to provide this type of after school support.

DAILY NEURO NUGGETS FOR A HEALTHY BRAIN AND BODY

In addition to sharing Neuro Nuggets with Students and Staff during morning announcements, share them in your daily social media posts and on the school website. Ideas and research referenced throughout this book are a great place to start. Ideas to consider range from our brain capacity and battery charge levels, to environmental influences such as sleep and exercise on healthy brain development and critical thinking, to how to establish routines in the home (pack backpacks and pick out clothes the night before, Monday/Wednesday/Friday eat eggs and toast for breakfast, Tuesday/Thursday eat cereal and fruit, etc.) to increase the efficiency of people living together. Julie has provided many Neuro Nugget Parent sessions around the world on these topics and Parents have expressed their appreciation as many are not aware of the fascinating research about the young brain and what it needs to succeed.

PARENT AND COMMUNITY SCHOOL SPIRIT CAMPAIGNS

Promote enthusiasm and school spirit by posting a question of the day on social media; people who respond are entered into monthly drawings to win school spirit wear and free entrance into school events.

RANDOM ACTS OF KINDNESS (RAK) CAMPAIGNS

Kindness increases happy chemicals in the brain and decreases stress. Share clips of research about this idea and promote RAK selfies to school social media accounts, using the school hashtag. Encourage Students, Parents, and Staff to participate also. Provide opportunities for Parents to learn about and engage with each other in learning more about powerful ways to relieve anxiety and stress such as exercise, laughter, deep breathing, art, and social connectedness.

STUDENT-PARENT-STAFF SUCCESS PACT

A simple pact that can be agreed upon by Parents, Students, and Staff, as to what each contributes to increase success, can serve as the foundation for who provides what in the home and school learning environments. Involve Parent, Student, and Staff voice in the wording of the agreement. Following is a sample:

Student-Parent-Staff Success Pact

- *Students will: complete assignments on time, ask for help when needed, practice a growth mindset by completing retakes when needed, and participate in at least one extracurricular activity throughout school year.*

- *Parents will provide a home environment where Student receives: at least nine hours of sleep each night, healthy food, one to two+ hours of physical activity daily, appropriate clothing, screen time limits, and at least 10 minutes each day engaging positively with Parent/s. Parents will cultivate growth mindset by praising effort, improvement, and actions, and attend at least one school event each month.*

- *Staff will: electronically post learning topics, assignments, due dates, and resources for extra help every two weeks, respond to Student and Parent support requests within 48 hours, support growth mindset by allowing students to revise work and retake assessments until proficiency is demonstrated, limit class lectures to 10 minutes, and use a variety of instructional methods that increase critical thinking and interaction throughout a lesson.*

ADVOCATE APPROPRIATELY

It can be difficult to deal with a Helicopter Parent, one who bombards us with continual emails, hallway conferences, or demanding voicemails. When we encounter this behavior, it is time to sit back, exhale, and remind ourselves that the Parent is just trying to do what he thinks is best for his Student.

This personal reminder should cue all sorts of other thoughts, though. For instance, if this is how the Parent truly believes he can best advocate for his Student, then he has no idea how to advocate. With this in mind, we absolutely cannot forgive ourselves the responsibility of teaching appropriate advocacy skills to our Parents, but we also want to clarify what each (Students, Parents, Staff) are responsible for in this relationship by incorporating some type of a Success Pact.

Welcome positive interaction between school and home and establish guidelines for Parent communication, for example:

> *Dear Parent,*
>
> *To maximize our efficiency in decreasing Student struggles, upon concern, first contact the person directly associated with the situation (teacher, administrator, etc.) PRIVATELY to discuss concerns and ideas for improvement. If concern is not remedied, follow up with an email or voicemail to this effect, "Thank you for speaking with me recently about my child's struggle with _____. We have been doing _____ at home, to improve in this area; however, he is still struggling. Can you please share further insight into this situation and more ideas in how to help him be more successful?"*
>
> *If the concern continues after those two communications, then please contact the next person in the chain of command and set up a face-to-face meeting with all involved.*

 # BE MINDFUL OF LANGUAGE AND CULTURAL BARRIERS

Collectively, schools often adjust to meet the diverse needs of a community. Second-language populations have increased dramatically in many areas over the past decade, and many schools have worked fervently to provide for large, diverse populations. However, small schools and schools with a small percentage of second language populations (less than 10 percent) may still need to make adjustments as their resources often are not the same as the larger districts, with more diverse demographics.

Consider the following ideas:
- Hire Staff with diverse skill sets and experiences.
- Provide cultural awareness training to Staff.
- Use community and Student translators as needed.
- Share support Staff with other districts.
- Utilize a translation app or tech tool, such as Duolingo or Google Translate.

 # UTILIZE COMMUNITY LIAISONS TO PARTNER WITH SECOND-LANGUAGE PARENTS

PJ's district has invested in hiring bilingual Community Liaisons for every school site, and it has completely transformed their ability to connect with families. The community liaison reaches out to Parents and creates bilingual engagement and learning opportunities at the school site WHILE building relationships. The liaisons partner with the social worker, teacher specialists, and local agencies to develop morning and evening workshops for families to support Maslow and Bloom needs.

Parent Liaison workshop topics include:
- Literacy and math
- Digital citizenship
- English language acquisition
- Health and wellness
- Gardening
- Mental health
- Positive Parenting strategies
- Classroom volunteering
- Leadership development: School Site Council, English Learner Advisory Council

 # INCREASE PARENT REACH

When we only allow face-to-face meetings or one-time offerings to busy Parents, then we may experience a low turnout. If experience shows less than 30 percent of Parents attend school events, then assess what you can do to increase attendance and interaction.

For instance, if you plan to offer a Parent informational night about bullying, but events such as this are typically not well attended, provide the following to increase your audience reach:

- A pre-event survey asking when is the best time to hold Parent workshops or events
- Language translation, as needed
- Personal invites from teachers or principal
- Food
- Childcare, with enrichment and homework help
- Articles and websites with additional resources
- Contact information of a person who can provide follow-up support
- Livestream via Periscope and Facebook Live
- A video of the event on YouTube and the school website

If you implemented just the last two bullet points, you would double your audience reach at NO additional cost. To increase the knowledge and availability of your resources, increase the ways in which you provide them.

#FULLYCHARGED WRAP-UP

To increase social-emotional ecstasy in the Parent brain and maximize our energy and resources, following are a few questions to guide your steps in meeting Parent Maslow needs:

- Who are your Parents, and what are their struggles and experiences?
- What types of Maslow resources and services can you provide at the school site?
- How do you meet Parent needs in: Parenting, Communication, Volunteering, Learning at Home, Decision-Making, and Collaboration?

Treating our Parents as partners by strengthening, caring for, and encouraging them allows us to foster home and school environments that help our Students to flourish.

#FULLYCHARGED

CHAPTER 3: BOOK STUDY/ TWITTER CHAT QUESTIONS

1. Describe a Parent you know whose Maslow needs are not being met. How does this influence the Student's success?

2. How does your school system identify and support Parent Maslow needs?

3. What are two principles from this chapter that will most influence how you interact with Parents?

4. Which two Battery Charging Strategies do you think would help Parents immediately?

5. Identify three ideas that resonate with you from this chapter. How will you share those ideas with your Students/Parents/Staff?

Please visit effectiveteachingpd.com or mbsimplesolution.com to watch the #FULLYCHARGED Author Chat about this chapter and participate in our 21 Day Challenge.

CHAPTER 4
Meeting Staff Maslow Needs

"Education is a profession that drains a lot of emotional energy. When our Staff is appreciated, strengthened, and #FULLYCHARGED on our campuses, they greatly increase the likelihood that our Students and Parents will be well cared for and #FULLYCHARGED as well. To grow Student Bloom's, cultivate Staff Maslow's."

—Julie Adams

∗   ∗   ∗   ∗   ∗

"'I bring me wherever I go.' I was co-presenting with a colleague at *AASA*'s National Conference on Education, when he made that statement. It's so simple, but it succinctly put what I always cognitively knew, though seldom acted on as an educational leader. I bring me wherever I go."

—PJ Caposey

During my first year as a school administrator, I (PJ) was working with one Teacher who was fighting cancer, another going through a messy divorce, and one more who was doing everything he could to battle deep depression. These people deserved empathy from their administration, their peers, and in some cases, even their Students. The overwhelming majority of the time they received it.

I remember multiple times though when my Staff accountability sensor would go off, and my instinct would be to have a direct conversation with each of the Staff, even the struggling ones, about fulfilling their responsibilities to our Students. I would remind myself to be empathetic, soften my approach and tone, and make sure that we provided the extra support they needed to be successful. All of us made it through the year, and the following year, those three who were really struggling even returned to all-star form. Success!

However, during that same year, my Student achievement accountability sensor went off, and off, and off. As a result, I went off, and off, and off. I was driven to raise outcomes for the traditionally low-performing and underprivileged kids that we served. I did not feel that I had time to wait, think, or consider others' feelings. The work simply needed to get done; even if we had personal struggles, we had to fulfill our professional duties.

Initiative after initiative, reform after reform, and mandate after mandate, I was dogged in my pursuit of improvement. I was completely unsympathetic of anyone else's thoughts or concerns as mine were keenly focused on providing a better product for our Students.

Oh, you do not like the direction we are moving? Great, I am sure you can find somewhere else where you are a better fit.

This is so much, so quickly that it is hard for you to keep up? Ok, you have two options: keep up or get out.

Well, guess what? We started to see minor improvements in achievement rather quickly. I thought I was vindicated. My push, push, push method worked. We "Best Practiced" everything, and I kept barking to get the ship moving in the right direction.

Then came the resignations, voluntary transfers, the acceptance of offers from other districts. They were leaving. Not just the ones that I wanted to leave, but everyone was leaving, or at least thinking about it.

My ego would not let me accept that this was a sign that my approach was not working. Then, one of the few Teachers who still liked me, or at least cared enough to tell me the truth, popped into my office. She reminded me that the cause was noble and the sense of urgency necessary, but I had gone too far. She reminded me that Staff "live there" and administration typically "just visits."

I was shook up and argued at first. We needed the results! We needed to do better by kids! So, I pushed forward, in retrospect, with my head in the sand. One night, a few weeks later, I was walking across campus, and I noticed one of my science Teachers still working in her classroom.

I poked my head into her classroom, thinking I should say something that showed my appreciation for her work ethic. Instead, I took that opportunity to mention that I noticed her Students were lined up at the door earlier that day, ready to leave her class long before the bell even rang, and I was not happy about it.

Before I could even get to the research supporting bell-to-bell teaching, the teacher broke down in tears. She explained that she was overwhelmed and working late for the next few weeks to get the rest of the year planned, because her spouse was being deployed and she would have extra responsibilities while he was away. Wow, that hit me right between the eyes.

The next day, I called in the Teacher who had the courage to try to "wake me up" a few weeks prior. I asked her to tell me who was going through some "real" stuff right now. She looked at me like I was crazy, but I persisted.

She shared how Mr. S is struggling with a custody issue, Ms. T is having financial troubles, Mr. C has a special-needs child who needed around-the-clock support, and my Staff's troubles kept tumbling out for several minutes.

In that moment, I learned empathy is for everyone. Empathy is not just for the few who may be fighting short-term hardships. Empathy is understanding that everyone has a long story, and most are more complicated and stressful than my own. Teachers are not widgets who can be programmed to regurgitate some curricula. They are human and need to be nurtured and cultivated. We are in the human *business.*

I finally got it, but I never knew how to say it. I could not articulate everything I felt about how we operated as humans and how we needed to operate with humanity, until my colleague said, "I bring me wherever I go."

We are professional educators, but we are humans first. Our Maslow needs must also be met before we can think about developing our pedagogical skills. Healthy cultures are borne out of a mutual respect and deep understanding that we are here to serve others for the long term, not just provide a short-term fix. We sleep more soundly at night and are more competent and confident when we serve others' needs instead of worrying about only our own. In other words, I am content with myself when I look to serve outside of myself.

✳   ✳   ✳   ✳   ✳

"I gave OF myself, but failed to give TO myself."

—Rosa Isiah

I (Rosa) was in elementary school when I decided to become a Teacher. Teachers were an incredible inspiration to this new-to-the-country English learner. I was welcomed and nurtured, and most Teachers made me feel as if I could achieve anything I wanted. School became my safe haven. I cried if I had to miss a day to help out at home or to translate at a doctor's appointment for my mom. I was a focused and dedicated Student, despite the challenges brought on by poverty and lack of opportunities. I knew by fifth grade that I would teach.

Soon after high school, I applied for an Instructional Assistant position at the very school I attended as a child. I was hired and honored to be part of the elementary school that inspired me to teach. At the time, I worked two part-time jobs, attended college part time, and attempted to rest and sleep whenever I could. Living at home, helping my family out on top of my workload, exhausted me.

I quickly realized how emotionally demanding and physically exhausting our profession can be. I was a 19-year-old, first-generation college Student attempting to balance my passion for education with my reality. I was constantly fatigued and falling behind in my college coursework. I worked at a school within my community, my home school, where Students came in with trauma and a variety of needs. I gave OF myself, but failed to give TO myself. My battery was DRAINED daily. Slowly, I began to lose my focus; I felt like a failure as an educator. How could I possibly care and nurture learning in others when I wasn't caring for myself?

After a few months as an Instructional Assistant, I realized something had to change. I was running on empty and got to a point where I was neglecting the basics: sleep, safety, stability. I had the passion for my work and loved being part of the Staff. But passion isn't enough when our physiological needs are neglected. I knew that if I wanted to achieve my dream of becoming a Teacher, I needed to make immediate changes. After an inspiring and honest conversation with my mentor Teacher, I decided to apply for a full-time job and to move out of my family's apartment. This full-time job meant I'd step away from my work as an Instructional Aide. It was difficult, but I knew I'd be back. The move allowed me more space and time to study and rest. My family was very supportive; they understood that I needed to care for myself first.

After a couple of years, I returned to my work as an Instructional Aide. I now had balance in my life, along with the passion to make a difference for Students. It was the same passion that I embraced when I first began my journey as an Instructional Assistant.

In order for Staff to reach their highest potential, we must take into consideration our own basic needs. This may require us to seek assistance and make life changes in order to achieve the highest level of self-actualization. Meeting our own needs will make us better for others.

*   *   *   *   *

"Meanwhile, a dozen other Students in my class were in need."

—Todd Finley

Todd Finley, educator and author, shared his experience with us:

"Caring is a finite resource." I learned that from an Ojibwe second-grader.

At the beginning of the school year, David would jerk his neck back to flick the bangs out of his light brown eyes and write, "I love Mario. I love Mario. I love Mario." to the bottom of the page, and then grin and ask, "What do you think, Mr. Todd?" Some days, the page would be filled with, "I love soccer."

In early October, David stopped playing soccer at recess. When I asked him why, he walked away. Then he stopped writing. Each week, he became more of a ghost, refusing to communicate with me. One day after school, David broke the lock on my desk and stole my stockpile of pens. I caught him selling them, 10 for a quarter. The boy's guardians never returned my urgent messages. Meanwhile, a dozen other Students in my class were in need.

The day before Thanksgiving break, the administrative assistant noticed David cupping his left ear in the cafeteria. I stopped breathing for a minute, suddenly awake to the fact that my Student had been covering his ear all week without me registering that he might be in pain. Nor had I noticed that David's previously white T-shirt was now the color of oatmeal and smelled like neglect.

When the administrator moved David's hand away, we saw that his ear canal had volcanoed into a mound of ooze and reddish-black crust. I was horrified by the wound and by my callousness, and ashamed to stand beside a colleague's full heart. Kneeling to hug the boy, she looked up at me and mouthed, "Oh my gosh!"

Fortunately, David flourished with a new guardian and counseling. And while there is no defending criminal disregard for a child in my care, I now realize that my emotions had narrowed to low levels, after working with children whose temper swings overwhelmed my meager skills.

Rocket Science Research

Todd Finley, educator and author of the above narrative, shares research about compassion fatigue, secondary traumatic stress, and strategies to overcome them in his Edutopia blog, "Are You At Risk for Secondary Traumatic Stress?":

"Any professional who listens to children recount traumatic experiences is at risk of secondary traumatic stress, the emotional weight that some teachers carry after exposure to children who suffer. According to the National Child Traumatic Stress Network, secondary traumatic stress degrades our professional effectiveness and overall quality of life. According to Sheri Brown Sizemore, author of To Love to Teach Again: 10 Secrets to Rekindling Passion to Keep You in the Classroom, *symptoms include anger, cynicism, anxiousness, avoidance, chronic exhaustion, disconnection, fear, guilt, hopelessness, hypervigilance, inability to listen, loss of creativity, poor boundaries, poor self-care, and sleeplessness.*

If you recognize these symptoms, complete the Professional Quality of Life Scale (http://proqol.org/uploads/ProQOL_5_English_Self-Score_3-2012.pdf), which measures compassion fatigue. Also be aware that there are strategies that can help, like these:

1. *Connect with quality friends: Every Thursday morning at 5:30, I show up in a music teacher's driveway for a 50-minute 'walk & talk.' Eddie and I always discuss teaching problems. Besides being a good listener, my friend reminds me that my feelings matter, and that I'm enough. Regardless of my difficulties, I end the walk feeling emotionally recharged.*

2. *Write it out: Teaching requires mental and emotional dexterity. When one is weakened, the other is compromised. But writing can help. According to research, expressive writing (describing feelings) '"offloads" worries from working memory, therefore relieving the distracting effects of worry on cognition' (https://www.health.harvard.edu/healthbeat/writing-about-emotions-may-ease-stress-and-trauma). Set a timer for eight minutes and let it all out on paper.*

3. *Use drive time for self-talk: If I'm feeling out of sorts while driving to work, I talk about my concerns aloud and in the third person. For example: 'Todd is feeling raw and fragile because of the crying jag that X had yesterday. He'll be OK today if he doesn't get overpowered by X's feelings.' This emotional distancing, according to research on third-person self-talk, boosts rationality and improves people's 'ability to control their thoughts, feelings, and behavior under stress' (http://selfcontrol.psych.lsa.umich.edu/wp-content/uploads/2014/01/KrossJ_Pers_Soc_Psychol2014Self-talk_as_a_*

regulatory_mechanism_How_you_do_it_matters.pdf). After that, I put Aloe Blacc's 'The Man' on full blast and float into my classroom.

4. Avoid toxic colleagues: Research shows that toxic co-workers 1) are selfish, 2) display overconfidence, and 3) are found to declare 'emphatically that the rules should always be followed no matter what' (https://news.harvard.edu/gazette/story/2015/11/those-toxic-co-workers/). If a toxic co-worker hangs out in the break room, eat elsewhere with colleagues who smile with their eyes.

5. Do something tangible: To avoid marinating in diminished compassion, recharge by completing a small task—something specific and concrete. Hop on an elliptical machine for 30 minutes or send a card to a friend. Teresa Amabile and Steven Kramer, authors of The Progress Principle: Using Small Wins to Ignite Joy, Engagement, and Creativity at Work, describe how small victories promote a more positive inner life, which 'also leads people to do better work.'

6. Don't suppress painful feelings: When I'm worried about a student, I remember that I don't have to be perfect and that there are weeks left to make a difference. 'Mastering the ability to reframe problems is an important tool for increasing your imagination because it unlocks a vast array of solutions' (https://www.fastcodesign. com/1672354/how-reframing-a-problem-unlocks-innovation). A good psychotherapist can help you reframe issues, boost your emotional resilience, and enhance your classroom effectiveness.

Finally, don't forget the most important thing. 'It's easy to say, "It's not my child, not my community, not my world, not my problem,"' said Fred Rogers. 'Then there are those who see the need and respond. I consider those people my heroes.' Don't forget who you are."

STAFF EFFICACY IMPACTS STUDENT EFFICACY AND ACHIEVEMENT

Researcher John Hattie, ranked teacher efficacy (competence and confidence) as the number-one influence on achievement. In other words, when the Staff believes they make a difference, they make a difference.

In the article "Fostering Collective Teacher Efficacy-Three Enabling Conditions," author Jenni Donohoo elaborates:

"Collective teacher efficacy, as an influence on student achievement, is a contribution that comes from the school—not the home and not the students themselves. According to the Visible Learning Research (Hattie, 2012), it is more than double the effect of prior achievement (0.65) and more than triple the effect of home environment (0.52) and parental involvement (0.49). This supports Bob Marzano's (2003) conclusion, *based on his analysis of research conducted over thirty-five years, that 'schools that are highly effective produce results that almost entirely overcome the effects of student backgrounds' (p. 7). Research shows that at the school level, collective teacher efficacy beliefs contribute significantly to the school's level of academic success."*

She provides three ways to increase collective competence and confidence:

- Advanced Teacher Influence
- Goal Consensus
- Responsiveness of Leadership

To increase Teacher influence, include Teachers in the decision-making process regarding culture and climate, professional development, curriculum, parental involvement, and so forth. To create goal consensus, gather Staff ideas, then establish measurable and achievable goals and the resources and support to attain them. Responsive leaders further grow Staff efficacy by being aware of obstacles that could prevent Teacher efficiency and diminishing them as necessary.

COMPETENCE AND CONFIDENCE ARE TRANSFORMATIONAL

The Leader in Me program, introduced in 2009 by Franklin Covey, has exploded in popularity and spread rapidly throughout the world. Currently, over 3,000 schools in over 50 countries have adopted this as a paradigm of execution. The program discusses five key paradigms that need to shift in order for education to truly transform (Figure 4-1).

- EVERYONE CAN BE A LEADER IN THEIR SCHOOL AND IN LIFE.
- EVERYONE HAS A GENIUS INSIDE WAITING TO BE REALIZED.
- EVERYONE HAS THE CAPACITY FOR GROWTH AND IMPROVEMENT.
- EVERYONE IS EMPOWERED AND CHALLENGED TO LEAD THEIR OWN LEARNING.
- SCHOOLS SYSTEMATICALLY FOCUS ON SERVING AND STRENGTHENING BOTH STUDENTS AND STAFF, EMOTIONALLY AND ACADEMICALLY.

FIGURE 4-1. FIVE KEY PARADIGMS

This efficacy mindset drives how the Staff treat, view, and embrace their own influence on Students. It's a #FULLYCHARGED effect when Staff believe and act according to these five principles.

The brilliance of *The Leader in Me* is that when you purchase the program, they do not come and set it up so it can be implemented. Instead, they spend an entire year working on developing leadership capacity within the Staff first. The concept of "You cannot teach, what you do not know" is at the forefront of their philosophy.

This program serves to recharge batteries and provides a model to educators who want to implement some of their ideas. The program forces reflection, addresses the whole person, and emphasizes the genius within all of us. But more than just a curriculum, it is a comprehensive approach to leadership development within a school. This model is now being replicated by other organizations for good reason. Their success is impressive because it develops both emotional and academic skill, or in other words, Maslow's and Bloom's.

IS ALL THIS REALLY NECESSARY IN OUR PROFESSION?

The "MetLife Survey of the American Teacher" notes that the stress of teaching is at an all-time high and nearly 50 percent will leave the profession within the first five years. So, we have two choices: attack the problem or cross our fingers and hope it goes away. If you are reading this book, you have probably chosen to attack the problem.

To solve this issue, we must acknowledge that resilience and social-emotional competency (SEC) are skills to be tilled, not unteachable talents. The same way schools focus on developing Staff pedagogical skill, so must we work toward meeting and developing their social-emotional aptitude. This is a firm acknowledgement that we are investing in the whole person, instead of an instructional robot.

Does this sound soft and fluffy to you? Dr. Lorea Martinez shares in her article, "Developing Teachers' Social and Emotional Skills," that striving to meet Staff Maslow needs is worth it because their social-emotional satisfaction also improves:
- Teacher-Student relationships
- The ability to monitor and develop Students' social-emotional competency
- Organization and classroom management skills

Education can be a draining profession; it is vital that we strengthen and encourage those who are in it so they achieve efficacy and can fulfill their potential in positively growing capacity in themselves and in our Students.

> "Train your people well enough so they can leave.
>
> Treat them so well that they don't want to."
>
> —Sir Richard Branson

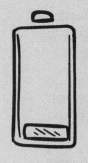

BATTERY CHARGING STRATEGIES
MEET STAFF MASLOW NEEDS AND GROW THE 5CS OF LEADERSHIP

To be #FULLYCHARGED and encourage social-emotional ecstasy in Staff, consider these strategies to cultivate competence, confidence, compassion, and creative, critical thinking.

WELLNESS COMMITTEES

Does your school have a Wellness Committee? They are common and focus on meeting the social-emotional Staff needs. Recruit a small, friendly group to spearhead four or five of the following ideas throughout the school year.

WALKING GROUPS

Any workout group is a great idea, but concepts such as running or crossfit can be intimidating to the masses. Therefore, a simple walking group can help spread the "fitness bug" and also provide an opportunity for Staff to form meaningful personal relationships with their colleagues.

BIGGEST "FAT" LOSERS

"The Biggest Loser" TV program is popular for a reason: people love to see others meet their health goals. While any activity that brings people together and encourages healthy behaviors is a benefit, it is important to make sure we are incentivizing the right behaviors. A contest to lose body fat is safer and healthier than one that just encourages people to drop weight. A phone call to a dietician or a personal trainer will almost certainly lead to "free" measurements to start this friendly competition.

TAP INTO HEALTH EXPERTISE

Health coaches, personal trainers, and dieticians appreciate the opportunity to speak to prospective clients. Partnering with a gym to provide short "Lunch and Learn" sessions at the school, video tutorials, and workout plans helps to create an atmosphere of fitness and health on the campus.

 BIOMETRIC SCREENINGS AND PHYSICALS

Most insurance companies will provide these assessments free of cost for school districts. Provide these opportunities during professional development days and incentivize participation through a raffle. This encourages people to have their health checked and also affirms the fact that we, as a school, value the health and well-being of the whole person.

 CHAIR MASSAGES

Invite in a massage therapist (or therapists in training) to provide 10-minute massages to help relieve stress. This is a non-intimidating way to introduce this stress reliever to those who have never tried it. This idea will be loved by some and avoided like the plague by others. The bottom line is that not every idea has to meet the Maslow needs of your entire Staff. We are recharging one battery at a time, so providing a variety of ways to meet needs is helpful.

 NEW TEACHER SUPPLY SHOWER

Host a lunchtime or afterschool get together similar to a baby shower, for your new Staff every year. Veterans can share on a Google Doc which classroom supply item they will be giving the newbie, to ensure they are blessed with a much-needed classroom toolkit full of various items such as glue sticks, markers, or post-it notes. Enjoy lunch, and share a few funny stories about first-year teaching to encourage and connect with new Staff.

 FINANCIAL SEMINARS

Financial stress seems to be omnipresent in our lives. Educators have worn the badge "I did not go into this to get rich" with pride, but doing so does not serve to fulfill our innate desire for financial security. Retirement and investment planning sessions are more than inviting a vendor in once to go over the details of potential investment opportunities. It is providing multiple opportunities to learn about options to help us make the most of our assets and do whatever we dream of doing in the present and in the future.

 # IN-SCHOOL DAYCARE

On top of several easy-to-form community partnerships, think how incredible and stress-relieving it would be to have this service available in your school or district. Many schools have started offering this as it is a convenient cost-saver for Teacher-Parents *and* a revenue-generator for the school. It can also be offered as an Early Childhood Career Tech Ed class that is overseen by preschool Staff and trained high school Students.

 # CAR SERVICE VALET

One of the hardest parts about being a career professional is the never-ending list of to-do's that exist once you get home. Nobody likes spending their weekends running errands. Just like large corporations are starting to offer their employees, creative schools can work to create meaningful community partnerships that systematically relieve Staff of stress. A simple idea is to offer periodic car service valet. Create a Google Doc for Staff to sign up on and partner with a local auto repair shop to come to the office, pick up the keys, and service and clean the car during the school day. When done, the repair shop (happy for the surge in business) drops off the vehicle and invoices the owner. This model can also be applied to dry cleaning and other common errands.

 # SUNSHINE CLUB

Most schools have some version of this already, but having an organized group whose sole intent is to provide fun, community-building activities at staff meetings and at other times throughout the year is very beneficial. As a side note, these work best when they are not administratively run and a great way to honor and leverage other forms of leadership within your building.

 # MANDATORY FUN

Now, this does not have to actually be mandatory, but it does have to be fun. Examples of group activities that increase fun are: laser tag, Top Golf or miniature golf, bowling, paint-and-sip nights, escape room challenges, ropes obstacle courses, 5K charity walks, Staff vs. Students Hula-Hoop competitions, and spirit days.

NO-WORK WEEKENDS

Periodically, make an agreement with Staff that they will not touch one work-related thing the rest of the weekend; then encourage them to share a few pics of fun things they are doing instead. Sometimes it's helpful to even offer half-day subs so Staff can complete the work they were going to do over the weekend during the work week. Few will take you up on the offer, but the offer is still a great way to let Staff know that it's okay to take the weekend off to recharge and have home and work balance.

 # CAREER COACHING AND COUNSELING

The greatest investment you can make in your Staff is not to view them as employees first, humans second. Simply seeing them for what they can become, instead of what they already are, opens tremendous dialogue and helps to transform the culture of a building. Ask each Staff member what their 5-, 10-, and 20-year career goals are, and offer resources to help them meet those goals.

 # MENTAL HEALTH AND SANITY SUPPORT

Consider a few of these ideas to support Staff sanity:

- Provide one-page summaries of IEPs.
- Have a quiet, confidential place for Staff to have a private conversation with a mental health professional.
- Play positive music over the intercom system between classes.
- Provide five- to eight-minute substitutes to fill in so a teacher can take a quick mental health walk around the building.
- Communicate this: "I appreciate you. Is there anything I can do to help you?"

 # SPEAK THEIR LANGUAGE

According to the book, *The 5 Languages of Appreciation in the Workplace*, everyone has a preference in how they like to be shown appreciation. We sometimes show others appreciation in the language WE prefer, but it may not be the way THEY prefer, so our gratitude may not be perceived correctly. The five languages are: Acts of Service, Words of Affirmation, Gifts, Physical Touch, and Quality Time. Before expressing gratitude, ask Staff how they prefer to be thanked. An Acts of Service person may appreciate assistance in gathering volunteers to help with the upcoming track meet; whereas, a Physical Touch person may just appreciate a smile and a pat on the back.

MEANINGFUL EVALUATION

If you haven't read PJ's book, *Making Evaluation Meaningful*, check it out! Formal Staff evaluations are our most systematic approach to investing in all employees. However, these are typically a battery drainer, not a battery charger, so we must do something different. What about having quarterly growth meetings with Staff to talk about what they want to talk about? One of PJ's Staff was great at her job, but she wanted to be a youth minister; that was her passion and what really recharged her battery. So, guess what they talked about during their quarterly growth meetings? Yep, her youth ministry, and those conversations strengthened her even more as a Teacher. Invest in people and help them become who they are called to be, even if it means they will be exiting your school system.

 # WHY REMINDERS

Being an educator is hard. Why? Because we grow leaders. We have the best jobs in the world; but as great as our profession is, we have to intentionally reconnect our people to their purpose. Nothing recharges our batteries more than remembering our why. Have Staff each create a visual reminder of their "why." It could be a picture, a paragraph, or a poem, and then corporately share them. Take a picture of each Staff's why, and then send them out periodically to Staff as reminders. You can use Boomerang to schedule them. PJ's colleague used this recharge strategy with Staff and also sent along this powerful message: "Your WHY is our WHY." We do not grow weary by WHAT we do; we grow weary when we lose sight of WHY we do what we do.

 # POSITIVITY POPS

Positivity is contagious and is established intentionally. Create systematic "pops" of positivity. Staff appreciations are a great way to start a staff meeting and incorporate positivity into our culture. Have student government post positive messages around the school and have the video production class create a monthly one-minute video that includes Students and Staff sharing their favorite activities and school memories, along with positive messages from community members and retirees. The Positivity Pops can be shared at faculty meetings, on social media, and on the school website.

#FULLYCHARGED
WRAP-UP

To increase social-emotional ecstasy in Staff and maximize our energy and resources, consider these questions to guide your steps in meeting Staff Maslow's needs:

- How will you assess your Staff Maslow's needs?
- What resources will you provide to meet those needs?
- How can you connect with Staff and work collaboratively to address each others' needs?

Education can be a draining profession. Whether it's dealing with secondary traumatic stress or financial strain, this profession is certainly not for the faint of heart. An intentional, comprehensive plan to meet Staff Maslow needs is a commitment to strengthening and encouraging them to be #FULLYCHARGED.

#FULLYCHARGED

CHAPTER 4: BOOK STUDY/TWITTER CHAT QUESTIONS

1. Describe a Teacher you know whose Maslow needs are not being met. How does this influence his/her professional abilities?

2. How does your school system identify and support Staff Maslow needs?

3. What are two principles from this chapter that will most influence how you support Staff?

4. Which two Battery Charging Strategies do you think would help Staff immediately?

5. Identify three ideas that resonate with you from this chapter.

Please visit effectiveteachingpd.com or mbsimplesolution.com to watch the #FULLYCHARGED Author Chat about this chapter and participate in our 21 Day Challenge.

SECTION 2
Got Skills?

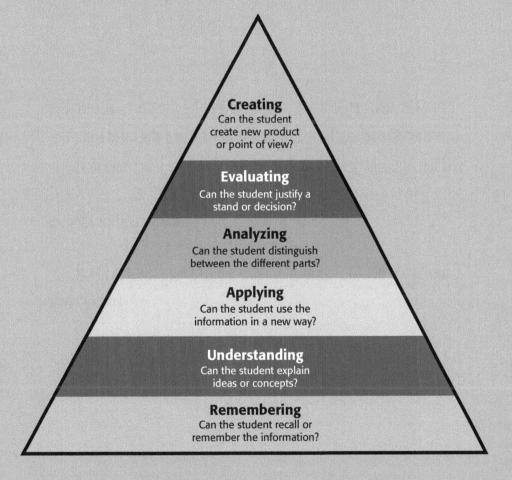

Creating
Can the student
create new product
or point of view?

Evaluating
Can the student justify a
stand or decision?

Analyzing
Can the student distinguish
between the different parts?

Applying
Can the student use the
information in a new way?

Understanding
Can the student explain
ideas or concepts?

Remembering
Can the student recall or
remember the information?

CHAPTER 5
Blooming Students

"Education must enable one to sift and weigh evidence, to discern the true from the false, the real from the unreal, and the facts from the fiction. The function of education, therefore, is to teach one to think intensively and to think critically."

—Martin Luther King, Jr.

"Education is not the learning of facts, but training the mind to think."

—Albert Einstein

*　　*　　*　　*　　*

"There is a difference between instructions and instruction. Students need both."

—Julie Adams

"Today class, we are practicing summarizing. It's a critical thinking and comprehension skill that is very helpful in the real world. As a teacher, I have often been asked to read an article about literacy strategies and summarize the ideas with my colleagues, or to compare two reading programs and summarize each to provide insight to our School Board as they discuss which to adopt for our district. I was even asked once by a hotel manager to summarize my enjoyable stay at their location to be used for their marketing.

Summarizing is an important skill to have, so for the next few days, we are going to practice it to describe what we learn in our history class about the American Revolution. To begin, read this short narrative about a young girl's experience during the Revolution and then summarize the main idea."

This was during the first few years of my teaching career and it was my first year teaching eighth grade. I (Julie) was teaching a three-period "Core" block of Reading, English, and U.S. History at a large middle school in California. My classes were the typical mixed-ability grouping with one third above proficient, one third proficient (or near), and one third below or far below proficient. Nearly half of them qualified for Free and Reduced Lunch, about 20 percent were second-language speakers, and two were diagnosed with severe emotional behavioral issues AND they were ALL expected to master the same set of standards.

Due to limited resources, there were no aides to help me traverse these treacherous waters either. It was just me and 33 adolescents who all deserved personalized attention, instruction, and engagement, but truthfully received very little of it.

The reality of our teaching situations sometimes reminds me of the saying, "Teaching is as easy as riding a bike, except the bike is on fire and your pants are on fire and everything is on fire—and the hose is trickling."

"Mrs. Adams, what do you mean 'summarize' the main idea? How am I supposed to know what the MAIN idea is, when there is so much shoved in there?"

"Johnny, stop screwing around. Just write a summary, and knock it off. You're in eighth grade, for goodness' sake; you should know how to identify and summarize the main idea."

"Mrs. Adams, no seriously. Teachers tell us to write summaries about stuff all the time, but when I do, I never earn a good grade. Everybody TELLS us to do it, but nobody SHOWS us how. So I AM being serious. How do I summarize?"

This Student was essentially saying, "Earn your dang paycheck, lady!"

Everybody assigns it; but few teach it.

It's right there as plain as day, and I was ashamed to admit it. I was committing assumicide.

How many times had I committed this to the detriment of my Students?

I was guilty of two things that drastically decreased Student success. First, I assumed this Student was wasting time by being snarky and questioning the assignment. Second, I assumed that he should have a certain skill set simply because he was of a certain age. These mindsets are still common in classrooms, though neuroscience shows that age doesn't determine skill set; experience and reflection do.

One of the reasons I was frustrated by Johnny's question was that I didn't know HOW to answer it. In truth, I didn't know how to teach a Student to summarize. I had never really thought about it, and I had never had a Student ask.

I told Johnny to read the passage again and write about the ideas that stuck in his mind, and they would probably be the main ideas to include in the summary. As I later read their summaries, though, it became clear that my suggestion was not effective, as many Students wrote about things that did not have anything to do with the main idea, even though they were things that "stuck" in their minds about the passage.

I was frustrated, deflated, and embarrassed that I didn't know how to help my Students be successful. During my prep, I walked through the Staff lounge and encountered two colleagues who taught the same classes as I. Nonchalantly, I started with, "Hey there, I was just wondering if you could tell me how to teach summarizing to a struggling Student?"

Teacher 1, with 20 years teaching experience, responded, "Sure, just tell him to write the main idea, or the important stuff, in a sentence or two."

Teacher 2, with four years experience, nodded but then added, "If that doesn't work, then I teach that a summary is what a news reporter provides for us about events, and we can do the same by answering the 'Reporter's Questions' of who, what, when, where, why, and how."

Teacher 1, who had more years teaching out of all of us, told me to do what I had already done with no success, so the number of years teaching does not necessarily equate to effectiveness. However, Teacher 2 taught me HOW to teach a skill set by applying it to the real world.

The next day, I went back into class and I apologized that I hadn't taught them the skill they needed, so we were going to learn and practice it together. I handed their summaries back to them and then showed them a clip of the previous night's news. We kept track of the who, what, when info that was provided, and then we put that information into two- to four-sentence summaries. We also revised the previous day's work.

I then asked them to practice playing the news reporter to summarize their favorite movie. Then we practiced this skill again with the American Revolution narrative, and something magical happened! It worked! I actually saw their light bulb come on about the skill of summarizing and how playing the role of a news reporter aids comprehension and critical thinking. We continued to "till the skill" for several days, and my Students were then able to read or watch an event and identify the main ideas by using the "Reporter's Questions" to summarize their learning.

Lessons learned?

- *I had many years of college and teacher training, yet I still lacked strategies for how to teach my Students the skills they needed.*
- *If it's not an innate trait, then till the skill.*
- *There is a difference between instructions and instruction. Students (and Staff) need both.*

We sometimes are guilty of not teaching general literacy and critical thinking such as summarizing, as we do specific critical thinking, such as solving linear equations. An effective math Teacher would probably not tell Students to solve linear equations without explaining, modeling, and guiding them through the process and then providing feedback about it, before having them do it on their own. We should employ those explicit methods to foster any type of skill set, including loading the dishwasher, answering the phone appropriately, and managing our digital citizenship.

That experience changed the way I viewed teaching in many ways.

First, teaching content AND critical thinking make the difference in developing skillful learners who can eventually be skillful and INDEPENDENT of me; which in turn, increases their competence, confidence, comprehension, and creative, critical thinking.

Next, I should not assume that a Student, regardless of age, knows how to critically think about content in order to comprehend the content, until I have provided explicit instruction, modeling, feedback, and practice in it.

Last, it schooled me in what my role is as an educator— which is about more than just building positive relationships with my Students. It's also to increase Students' skills and not give up until that happens. I was reminded of the John Wooden quote: "You haven't taught it until they have learned it."

"He now focused on learning, instead of just achieving a grade."

—PJ Caposey

Anthony was a student that I (PJ) knew; he attended an award-winning school in an affluent suburb of Atlanta. His Parents were both successful, college-educated professionals, and strong supporters of the school that Anthony and his FIVE siblings attended. Anthony was the second youngest and different than his siblings.

The rest of the Trissler boys and girls were exceptionally bright AND exceptionally strong at playing the "game" of school. As a result, earning A's was the norm and the firm expectation in the Trissler household.

Around the fifth grade, Anthony began to notice that he was different than his siblings. Unlike them, he found that he had to work really hard to maintain an A in math; he often struggled with understanding the content. He would typically score in the 70s on assessments, but do all of his homework and extra credit to ensure his grade never dipped below 90 percent.

AND Anthony did it! He maintained this progress, and although he sensed he was a little different than his siblings, nobody could tell. On paper, he was just another one of the Trissler kids, one of those Students the Staff would fight over to have added to their class lists.

Then came Algebra II during his 10th grade year. Anthony fought through Algebra in middle school and Geometry made sense to him, but then his elaborate charade of "playing" school and working the system for A's was finally outed.

Anthony definitely knew he was different from his family now. He was struggling intensely. He expected to have to work for his grades, but this was too much. Anthony was not only struggling, but his grade dipped to an F about 12 weeks into first semester. Never before had Anthony spent so much time studying or trying to work the system, but he simply did not have the skills to make this work.

The Trissler Parents intervened. They met with the Teacher. They studied with their child. They took away privileges, but nobody could understand how an A student could transform to an F Student, seemingly overnight. They all worked in partnership with the Teacher and slowly they started to see progress.

Anthony needed entire chunks of content retaught. His Parents were dumbfounded. How could he have "earned" an A in earlier classes when he knew none of the most important content? Anthony must have simply forgotten how to do certain things.

Anthony's Teacher, who happened to be married to a Math Teacher at the Junior High, reached out to see if they still had any of his old assessments. Luckily, the entirety of every assessment given during his seventh and eighth grade years were still available.

A closer look at the data shocked Anthony's Parents. He had not forgotten anything. He simply never learned it. Anthony was consistent in the scoring on almost every assessment. He would do great on the simple, low-level questions and do just enough to gain half points on some of the more complex problems without ever really demonstrating that he knew what he was doing. This happened over and over again.

After analyzing this data, his Teacher remediated those skills, provided additional instruction and practice, and leveraged online resources such as Khan Academy, and Anthony caught up in no time. Not only did his grade improve, but so did his understanding. What didn't make sense in seventh and eighth grade now clicked for him, which filled in the gaps he was missing in his higher-level coursework. Most important, Anthony no longer thought of himself less than or different than his brothers and sisters. He now focused on learning and improving with practice, instead of just achieving a grade.

The issue with Anthony's experience is that grades were considered feedback. While in the most generic sense of the word, this may be accurate, grades alone often do not provide adequate feedback to fuel improvement. The overvaluing of this type of feedback created a Student whose paradigm was focused on grade attainment, instead of learning. He developed a fixed mindset and thought there was nothing he could do to improve; therefore, his competence and confidence decreased.

For Anthony, a Teacher who invested in him as a person and provided specific feedback about his learning changed his academic trajectory, as he worked toward proficiency. His Algebra II Teacher saw time as a variable and learning as the non-negotiable and not the opposite (time = fixed, learning = negotiable) model too present in today's schools. She then made him think and then revise his thinking and did not allow him to progress without a deep understanding of how to solve the "difficult" problems. She leveraged every resource available, and she made a difference.

The investment his Teacher made in him initially helped Anthony grow as a Student, but he ultimately became #FULLYCHARGED after developing the competence, confidence, and critical thinking he needed for success.

> "As long as she could remember, she was told she was gifted and tremendously smart."
>
> —Rosa Isiah

I (Rosa) met Rosie when she was a bright nine-year-old who loved school. Rosie was one of just a few in her class who could not memorize her multiplication facts. She felt as if she was the only fourth-grader on the planet who didn't know what 7 x 6 was. Rosie tried everything she could to memorize her multiplication facts. She wrote them over and over, pages and pages of perfectly aligned math facts. She made beautiful bright flash cards. She asked her sisters to quiz her, but nothing helped. She felt like a complete failure, feelings she wasn't used to feeling.

Rosie's Parents weren't very worried at first and encouraged her to keep practicing. They were confident that Rosie would master those facts; she was a great Student, after all. She loved learning and was a great listener in class. She turned in her homework every day. Rosie wasn't used to not knowing *and began to have doubts about her intelligence. As long as she could remember, she was told that she was gifted and tremendously smart. But she wondered, if she was so smart, why couldn't she memorize a bunch of simple facts?*

Rosie's school experiences were also teaching her to have a fixed mindset about her ability to learn as she grew more discouraged with every failing quiz. The look of disappointment on her Teacher's face when she handed Rosie her multiplication facts quiz was the hardest for Rosie. She began suffering from stomachaches and chose not to participate in class discussions. Rosie didn't want to continue to disappoint her Parents or her Teachers, and she wished she could just disappear.

Mrs. McDonald, her Teacher, noticed the change in her behavior. She was concerned about her math struggles, though many struggled with memorization. Mrs. McDonald understood that memorization did not measure intelligence or reflect a Student's true math abilities. Mrs. McDonald was growth-minded and knew that Rosie could master the challenge. She met with Rosie, and they came up with an intervention plan to increase her success. Rosie shared how the math quizzes triggered extreme anxiety in her. Mrs. McDonald reminded her that knowing the math facts are useful and efficient, but more than anything, the goal was to help Rosie truly understand and own the concept of multiplication.

They met twice a week before school for a six-week round of individualized interventions. She reviewed a number of basic mathematical operations and strategies in a way that made sense to Rosie. They played math games, they read stories that included math concepts, and they took the strategies they learned and applied them to real life. How many pizzas would they need for the class party if every student received two slices of pizza? How many cases of water bottles would the grade level need if each case contained 24 bottles and there were a total of 96 fourth graders?

Multiplication finally made sense to Rosie. The individualized support that Mrs. McDonald offered not only helped Rosie become a stronger mathematician, but it made her feel safe and eased her anxiety about Math.

Blooming our Students often requires that we take a step back and differentiate instruction for them. Rosie's struggle felt like an unconquerable challenge to her, especially as a Student with a fixed mindset who was used to always "getting it right." With a little help from her Teacher, she was able to move beyond basic Bloom's memorization and recall of math facts into application and analysis of multiplication.

Fourth grade ended on a positive note for Rosie; she was #FULLYCHARGED!

Rocket Science Research

When it comes to determining what separates a good Teacher from a great one in the Bloom realm, the elemental difference is that a great one teaches both content AND critical thinking.

Many of us have heard a colleague lament, "I have too much math or science content to teach, so I don't have time to teach critical thinking!"

Yikes! If a Teacher believes his only role is to teach information, then he can be easily replaced by Google, sadly dooming Students to mediocrity, at best.

TEACHING only occurs when LEARNING happens. TEACHING = LEARNING.

The idea that "we are drowning in information, but starved for knowledge" is particularly true today. To turn information into knowledge so learning occurs, critical thinking, connection, and reflection must happen! That is why explicit modeling, feedback, and practice in the Bloom areas are so critical in developing independent critical thinking capacity.

In essence, "a masterful teacher is less necessary at the end of the course than at the beginning."

It is true that our Staff must teach content; however, the ultimate goal is to teach Students WHAT to do with the content so it sticks and makes sense. It has been said that our goal is not to teach Students WHAT to think, but to teach them HOW to think.

But HOW do we do that?

In the neuroscience world, this is referred to as improving executive function. While executive function is often described as critical thinking, that leaves a somewhat incomplete picture, but cues us into the greater meaning and desire of why improving executive functioning is so important in the ever-changing world.

Executive function takes place in the pre-frontal cortex of the brain, and while maturation in this region continues into our 20s, the most rapid development takes place between the ages of eight and the mid-teens.

Building Students' executive function skills provides the ability to critically analyze, judge, use inductive, deductive, and relational thinking, and increase their ability to predict. These are all necessary (and desirable) skills in the workplace.

The path to becoming a better facilitator of executive functioning begins precisely when our marriage to simply memorizing information is abandoned. Though there is a time and place for learning math facts and states and capitals, when Teachers make the switch from mainly just recall to focusing on the development of understanding, application, analysis, evaluation, and creation, then Students increase their likelihood of acquiring knowledge and skills in a way that sticks.

This is why it is valuable to develop Bloom's Taxonomy skills.

The path to activating the pre-frontal cortex and maximizing the impact of our time in the classroom has been influenced by educational research. Education is one of the most widely researched fields, and a strong body of research has been produced to guide practitioners in making decisions that strengthen Students' abilities IF we pay attention to it.

WHICH STRATEGIES WORK?

The Mount Rushmore of 21st century educational research contains namely two faces: Robert Marzano and John Hattie. Their contributions cannot be overstated to quantify the science of teaching, in order to provide guides for better teaching and learning. Marzano, Hattie, and their respective teams created complex and data-rich guides for effective instruction based on the statistical process of meta-analysis. While there is no singular "golden ticket" strategy per se, there are several for us to utilize to grow critical thinking capacity.

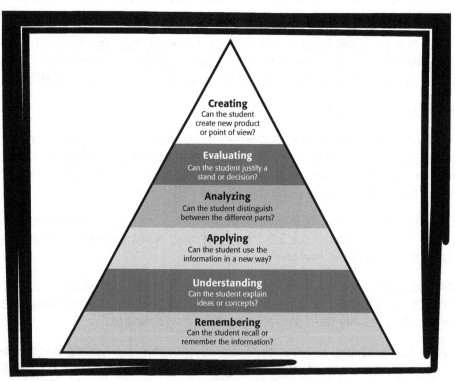

FIGURE 5-1. BLOOM'S TAXONOMY

Robert Marzano's book, *Classroom Instruction That Works*, highlights research that supports the teaching of nine best practices that increase comprehension and critical thinking:

- Identifying similarities and differences
- Summarizing and note-taking
- Reinforcing effort and recognizing growth
- Homework and practice
- Non-linguistic representations
- Cooperative learning
- Identifying objectives and providing feedback
- Generating and testing hypotheses
- Cues, questions and advance organizers

When in doubt, these nine strategies are a great place to start to increase critical thinking and connection to content; the clarity and research in that book are the reason it is widely used in teaching credential programs around the world. Applying Marzano's nine strategies into Bloom's Taxonomy is also a great way to identify which strategies can be foundational system-wide.

John Hattie's book, *Visible Learning*, synthesized over 800 meta-studies related to Student achievement and identified 138 strategies and their effect on learning. His recommendations have since been updated to include research from over 1200 meta-studies and 195 practices and their effects on achievement in "The Applicability of Visible Learning to Higher Education."

The issue with these two giants in the industry is that their conclusions do not directly align. This leaves us with two data-rich projects that are sometimes leading educators in different directions. What a conundrum!

In our attempt to bring easy-to-understand and accessible research to maximize your cognitive capacity so you can serve others, we've identified overlapping strategies found to have maximum impact in both studies that can be explicitly taught to our Students. In the Battery Charging section of this chapter, we provide several actionable strategies to leverage what we know works.

Largest Yield-Strategies
(as agreed upon by Marzano and Hattie)

Positive Teacher-Student
Relationships and Interactions

Forced critical thought (Embrace Bloom's)

Active engagement in the lesson
(Student-Centered Instruction)

Providing meaningful feedback
and allow for metacognition

Collaborative approach to learning

Systematic approach to building efficacy

Clear focus for the lesson

FIGURE 5-2. LARGEST YIELD STRATEGIES

Both Hattie and Marzano agree that positive Teacher-Student relationships are the foundation of success. In the article, "Relating to Students: It's What You Do That Counts," Robert Marzano states, "Positive relationships between teachers and students are among the most commonly cited variables associated with effective instruction. If the relationship is strong, instructional strategies seem to be more effective. Conversely, a weak or negative relationship will mute or even negate the benefits of even the most effective instructional strategies."

If our goal is to increase Student learning and success in order to grow leadership capacity, then we must first recognize that one of the most effective critical thinking strategies is fostering safe and positive relationships with our Students.

Therefore, Maslow-based strategies increase the effectiveness of Bloom strategies, and that combination has a profound impact on achievement.

INTELLIGENCE VS. CRITICAL THINKING

Scientific American published an article titled, "Why Do Smart People Do Foolish Things? Intelligence Is Not the Same as Critical Thinking and the Difference Matters." The author, Dr. Heather Butler, shares how intelligence is often associated with knowledge though IQ tests often measure skills such as visual and spatial awareness and informational recall, not content skills knowledge. It is possible to have a high IQ, but not have critical thinking. Though some no longer put much stock in IQ scores, occasionally Parents will talk about their Student's high IQ, yet question why it doesn't always correlate to judicious reasoning. Dr. Butler explains why this can be common:

> *"The advantages of being intelligent are undeniable. Intelligent people are more likely to get better grades and go farther in school. They are more likely to be successful at work. And they are less likely to get into trouble (e.g., commit crimes) as adolescents. Given all the advantages of intelligence, though, you may be surprised to learn that it does not predict other life outcomes, such as well-being. You might imagine that doing well in school or at work might lead to greater life satisfaction, but several large scale studies have failed to find evidence that IQ impacts life satisfaction or longevity. Grossman and his colleagues argue that most intelligence tests fail to capture real-world decision-making and our ability to interact well with others. This is, in other words, perhaps why 'smart' people, do 'dumb' things.*
>
> *The ability to think critically, on the other hand, has been associated with wellness and longevity. Though often confused with intelligence, critical thinking is not intelligence. Critical thinking is a collection of cognitive skills that allow us to think rationally in a goal-orientated fashion, and a disposition to use those skills when appropriate. Critical thinkers are amiable skeptics. They are flexible thinkers who require evidence to support their beliefs and recognize fallacious attempts to persuade them. Critical thinking means overcoming all sorts of cognitive biases (e.g., hindsight bias, confirmation bias, etc.)."*

It makes sense then to develop critical thinking skills, in addition to rote memorization of information, as knowing information does not mean one has the skills to apply the information in appropriate contexts, or even use it for gain. Having information without critical thinking and contextual connection capacity may look similar to the absent-minded professor portrayal. Those with higher critical thinking skills experience fewer negative life events, due to their better decision-making. The "Halpern Critical Thinking Assessment" is commonly used and tests skills in five areas: verbal reasoning, argument analysis, thinking as hypothesis testing, likelihood and uncertainty, and problem-solving. This assessment is used across industries to determine strengths and areas for growth, and often referenced when determining critical thinking abilities.

CULTIVATING CRITICAL THINKING

Researchers contend that critical thinking skills are an art and a science and though complex, they can and should be taught.

Dr. Eric Jensen writes in *Teaching With the Brain in Mind*: "Critical thinking skills take time to learn because you're asking the brain to make changes in both cortical organization and interregional connectivity. Learning new skills literally reorganizes brain mass…they have to be taught as part of a well-thought-out curriculum" (116).

He recommends skill development in the following areas:
- Maintaining focus and attention
- Locating and prioritizing resources
- Reading and summarizing content
- Distinguishing relevance and sequential order
- Comparing and contrasting
- Being able to speak about and draw non-linguistic representations
- Setting goals and providing descriptive feedback
- Having self-awareness of health and nutrition
- Generating and testing hypotheses
- Developing working memory capacity
- Being able to organize and map out ideas
- Showing persistence through struggle

In "Critical Thinking: Why Is It So Hard to Teach?" cognitive psychologist Daniel Willingham notes that the National Center on Education and Economy, The American Diploma Project, and The Aspen Institute are all in agreement that critical thinking can be difficult to teach, but success increases when it is combined with content knowledge:

> *"For example, an important part of thinking like a historian is considering the source of a document—who wrote it, when, and why. But teaching students to ask that question, independent of subject matter knowledge, won't do much good. Knowing that a letter was written by a Confederate private to his wife in New Orleans just after the Battle of Vicksburg won't help the student interpret the letter unless he knows something of Civil War history."*

Dr. Willingham also recommends teaching strategies explicitly and providing several opportunities for practice and revision; skill development is not a "one and done" occurrence.

> *"Critical thinking strategies are abstractions. A plausible approach to teaching them is to make them explicit, and to proceed in stages. The first time (or several times) the concept is introduced, explain*

it with at least two different examples (possibly examples based on students' experiences, as discussed above), label it so as to identify it as a strategy that can be applied in various contexts, and show how it applies to the course content at hand. In future instances, try naming the appropriate critical thinking strategy to see if students remember it and can figure out how it applies to the material under discussion. With still more practice, students may see which strategy applies without a cue from you."

Pearson Publishing released a meta-analysis, "Critical Thinking: A Literature Review" and concluded that critical thinking skills can be explicitly taught, improved with practice, and best learned when intertwined with content:

"Critical thinking includes the component skills of analyzing arguments, making inferences using inductive or deductive reasoning, judging or evaluating, and making decisions or solving problems. Background knowledge is a necessary but not a sufficient condition for enabling critical thought within a given subject. Critical thinking involves both cognitive skills and dispositions. These dispositions, which can be seen as attitudes or habits of mind, include open and fair-mindedness, inquisitiveness, flexibility, a propensity to seek reason, a desire to be well-informed, and a respect for and willingness to entertain diverse viewpoints. There are both general and domain-specific aspects of critical thinking. Empirical research suggests that people begin developing critical thinking competencies at a very young age. Although adults often exhibit deficient reasoning, in theory all people can be taught to think critically. Instructors are urged to provide explicit instruction in critical thinking, to teach how to transfer to new contexts, and to use cooperative or collaborative learning methods and constructivist approaches that place students at the center of the learning process.

In constructing assessments of critical thinking, educators should use open-ended tasks, real-world or 'authentic' problem contexts, and ill-structured problems that require students to go beyond recalling or restating previously learned information. Such tasks should have more than one defensible solution and embed adequate collateral materials to support multiple perspectives. Finally, such assessment tasks should make student reasoning visible by requiring students to provide evidence or logical arguments in support of judgments, choices, claims, or assertions."

These quotes reinforce the idea that effective teaching is a combination of content AND skills instruction and when we provide both, we help Students develop the tools for success.

GROWING CREATIVITY

One of the biggest myths about creativity is that it's a gift given to few. But this couldn't be further from the truth. We appreciate the following quotes about creativity:

> "Being creative does not mean you have to 'be an artist.' Being creative is about expressing yourself, and the more we express ourselves, the more good we create in the world."
> —Christine Mason Miller

> "Creativity involves breaking out of established patterns in order to look at things in a different way."
> —Edward de Bono

> "Creativity is intelligence having fun."
> —Albert Einstein

> "A great teacher is one who realizes that he himself is also a student and whose goal is not to dictate the answers, but to stimulate his students' creativity enough so that they go out and find the answers themselves."
> —Herbie Hancock

Creativity is the ability to analyze different methods to create and express new ideas and solutions. The more we practice, the better we become.

Cognitive psychologist Robert Sternberg states that creativity requires bravery, or competence and confidence, which comes from practice, mistakes, and revision. He shares in his article, "The Nature of Creativity," published in the *Creativity Research Journal*, to create a habit of creativity, practice these four ideas regularly:
- Look for ways to see problems (and solutions) that others don't.
- Take risks.
- Have the courage to defy the common belief.
- Seek to overcome obstacles that others give into.

Critical thinking and creativity are skills to be tilled. But how do we do it? Some Students drain their batteries in class because they simply do not know what to do with all of the information they receive. We can strengthen, encourage, and care for them by explicitly teaching a toolkit of creative, critical thinking strategies they can utilize with both fiction and non-fiction, in order to to flex their creative thinking and reflection capacity and turn information into knowledge. These strategies do not require fancy graphic organizers. Students can write them on binder paper, practice them verbally with a partner, or incorporate them using their tech devices.

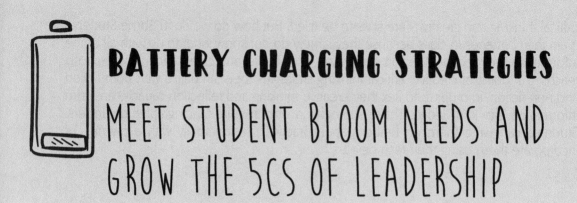

BATTERY CHARGING STRATEGIES
MEET STUDENT BLOOM NEEDS AND GROW THE 5CS OF LEADERSHIP

Consider these strategies to get Students #FULLYCHARGED with the SKILLS that cultivate competence, confidence, compassion, and creative, critical thinking.

 ## #READING

Students read two to four paragraphs of content and then #hashtag an important comprehension word from that section. Then #hashtag another important word from that section and then #hashtag a three- to five-word phrase that summarizes the section; it can be a direct quote or personal paraphrase. Repeat this process throughout a reading, and then have Students put all of their #hashtag responses together to create a summary "tweet" about the topic or sketch and add an image for the summary to "Instagram" it.

 ## L.I.S.T.E.N. TO LEARN

Active listening means paying attention to information to interpret and connect to it, so understanding occurs. Practice the acronym to improve listening skills:

Look interested by leaning in and making eye contact.

Involve your thinking by linking the idea to something you already know.

Stay focused by summarizing the main idea.

Test your understanding by asking a "how" or "why" question.

Evaluate the idea by asking yourself if you agree or disagree and why.

Neutralize your evaluation, or bias (for a period of time), to hear the entire message.

NEWS REPORTER

While learning a topic, have Students summarize the main idea by writing one sentence about each who, what, when, where, why, and how idea. Have them put the sentences into a summary paragraph and then rehearse the paragraph as if they were going to report it on the evening news. It's fun for Students to practice reciting the paragraph using various inflections such as Minnie Mouse or Buzz Lightyear.

 # SPACED AND SHARED RETRIEVAL

Throughout a lesson, have Students stop and retrieve (recall) two to four specific facts and restate the ideas in their own words. Then have them share their recall with another and compare, sketch an idea out, or create a mind-map about the concepts. Have them practice with information learned the previous day and week also. The more a piece of information is retrieved, the stronger the neural pathway to accessing that information becomes.

 # STUDENT GOAL-SETTING

Achievement increases when Students learn to set their own goals, practice metacognition, think about their thinking and progress, and have a clear understanding of the process needed to be successful. This concept is explored in depth in PJ's book (co-authored with Todd Whitaker), *Teach Smart: 11 Learner-Centered Strategies That Ensure Student Success.*

Have Students answer the following questions on an index card:

- What is my goal?
- What is my current level of proficiency in this area?
- Which strategies will I employ to meet my goal?
- Where can I get extra support to meet my goal?
- How will I know when I've reached my goal?

Using these questions to set academic goals, such as improving a math concept proficiency from 80 to 90 percent, can be extremely helpful. We can apply this principle to tie Maslow and Bloom success together as well:

> *"I want to increase the amount of sleep I get during the school week. I only get about five hours per night now, which is low compared to the 9 to 13 hours recommended, and I'm often too tired to concentrate in class. To sleep better, I will eliminate my afternoon caffeinated drink, exercise*

for at least one hour per day, and shut off my technology one hour before bedtime. I will talk to my mom about my goal and ask for her help if I still have trouble getting enough sleep. I will know when I have met this goal when I get at least nine hours of sleep each school night, for at least three weeks in a row, and am able to focus better in my classes."

 # TEACH WHAT GOOD CRITICAL THINKERS ASK

Albert Einstein shared this idea, "If I had an hour to solve a problem, I'd spend 55 minutes thinking about the proper questions to ask, for once I know the questions, I could solve the problem in less than five minutes." Teach Students what good critical thinkers ask and provide hot topic claims for them to practice with such as: Should the death penalty be eliminated? Should middle and high schools start after 9 a.m.? Should human cloning be legalized?

Critical thinkers:

- Make connections between claims: *How does this claim relate to another?*
- Evaluate claims for accuracy and relevance: *Is this statement accurate and connected to the claim?*
- Identify inconsistencies in reasoning: *Do these ideas support the claim?*
- Do not base their decisions on emotion but on facts and causal connection: *It's not whether I agree/disagree; what are the facts to support this claim?*
- Utilize information from more than one source: *Where can I get more reliable information about this claim?*
- Analyze ideas on both sides of the claim: *Who supports this claim and why? Who does not and why?*

 # CREATIVE CLOSURE

After learning about a fiction or nonfiction event, have Students rewrite or sketch a new ending for the event. Then have them compare and contrast the new and original endings, and share how this new version would have influenced the event.

 # TEACH WHAT GOOD READERS DO

Julie shares insight into explicitly teaching critical thinking strategies in her book *Game Changers: 7 Instructional Practices That Catapult Student Achievement.* She discusses 10 effective strategies that skilled readers utilize that we can train ALL Students in to increase their comprehension success:

- Re-read: *If I don't understand, I need to stop and re-read the section one to three more times because every time I re-read a section, I can learn more about it...*
- Read more slowly and stop after every section to complete a comprehension task: *If I don't understand, I should slow down and ask myself if I can identify at least one to two ideas the author is writing about...*
- Pre-read: *What can I learn from the title, subheadings, pictures, etc.?*
- Predict: *Based on my pre-reading, I think this will be about...*
- Connect to prior knowledge: *I already know _____ about this topic...*
- Visualize: *When I read this, I picture in my mind...*
- Question the text/author: *Why/What/How did the author...?*
- Retell: *First...Then...Finally...*
- Summarize: *Who/What/Where/When/Why/How?*
- Read the comprehension questions and/or summary first: *I can focus my attention and learn more by reading the questions and/or summary first...*

SELF-ADVOCATE

Teach Students to advocate for themselves in a professional and positive manner. Self-advocacy means that one can identify:

- What is needed to succeed: *What do I need to be successful: more time, practice, or more help from a tutor?*
- Who or what can provide those needs: *Who can help me in getting these needs met: a teacher, parent, counselor?*
- How to communicate those needs in a positive manner: *How can I communicate my needs in a positive manner, so others will want to help me?*

Example self-advocacy prompt to practice with Students:

> *"Mrs. Adams,*
>
> *I am struggling with my persuasive essay/linear equations/science homework, etc. I don't understand how to _____. I have already tried _____ and _____ to learn more, but I'm still struggling. Can you please help me or tell me where I can get extra support in this topic?*
>
> *Thank you,*
>
> *Jenny Smith"*

LAST LESSON, LAST WEEK, LAST MONTH

Educator and blogger Blake Harvard (theeffortfuleducator.com) shares this strategy:

"Provide questions (usually around three) from the last lesson, the last week, and the last month. Outside of letting students know what they know and what they've forgotten, this is particularly good for discussing common threads throughout lessons and units, tracing back to material covered a month or more in the past. Often, students see different units/chapters of a class as being 'stand-alone' and fail to understand how one concept in math or one event in history connects to what we're discussing today."

L.E.A.R.N TO RETAIN

Critical thinking increases when Students L.E.A.R.N. a concept. Teach them to:

Link to prior knowledge: What do I know about this concept already?

Evaluate: What is the most important idea and why?

Analyze: Which parts of this concept are connected to other concepts?

Retell: What happened first, second, finally?

Need to know: What is one more thing I need to know about this idea to better understand it?

NEWS FLASH

Students write a one-sentence summary, 20 words exactly, to synthesize their learning about a concept. The Teacher can provide two to four "focus words" or important content words, to include in the News Flash summary, to help identify the main idea and also increase the use of the content vocabulary.

3-2-1

Students write *three* facts learned, compare and contrast *two* ideas, and identify *one* new vocabulary term with the definition.

REFLECT TO BLOOM

Practice these Bloom's Taxonomy reflective ideas with Students:

- Remember: What was the assignment and did I turn it in (completed) on time?
- Understand: Did I understand the assignment and how it connected to the concept?
- Apply: How can I apply what I learned to other concepts?
- Analyze: What strategies did I use to understand the concept and do I need to make changes to increase my proficiency?
- Evaluate: Was I effective in developing AND sharing my knowledge about this concept?
- Create: How can I use the knowledge and skills I learned to create more success in my life?

INSTEAD OF DESPICABLE ME... EMPLOYABLE ME

What are employers looking for? Surprisingly, it's more "Will" than "Skill." In fact, many leadership programs recommend to employers that if they have to choose, they should hire Will over Skill and then provide job-specific Skill training. Raise Student awareness about the importance of developing the following employable skills: positivity, the ability to learn and receive feedback, responsibility, good hygiene, collaboration, face-to-face eye contact and appropriate body language, resourcefulness, collegial communication, and general analysis and problem-solving abilities.

FOCUS AND CONCENTRATION

Practice focused (mindful) breathing: teach Students to stop periodically throughout the day, focus on one item or activity they enjoy, such as a pet or playing a sport, and concentrate on that one thing as they slowly inhale for five seconds, then exhale for five seconds. Practice this concentration strategy for one to two minutes a few times per week.

The hippocampi, which are two areas in the brain responsible for critical thinking and retention, love one thing: oxygen-rich blood flow. Throughout the day, we are often rushed and stressed, and one of the first things to decrease is oxygen-rich blood flow to our hippocampi. Focused, deep breathing can improve concentration and critical thinking because it engages and strengthens the hippocampi, increases attention span, and decreases stress.

#FULLYCHARGED WRAP-UP

As mentioned in the narratives, whether your Students need explicit instruction in how to summarize, more descriptive feedback instead of just a letter grade, or real-world connections in order to understand concepts, you probably agree that they need both instruction and instructions in creative, critical thinking.

Instead of assigning the common ho-hum set of comprehension questions to Students (which do not foster independence), teach Students strategies that allow them to develop their own toolkit that cultivates independence and creative, critical thinking. Once they have mastered several tools, allow them to choose two to three to use while learning new material to practice their own metacognition: one Student may choose to use #Reading and News Flash while learning about photosynthesis or The Boston Massacre, while another uses 3-2-1 and News Reporter. Either way, they are flexing their thinking muscles and developing competence and confidence to turn information into knowledge.

Critical thinking and creativity are skills we can practice to improve success. If you're wondering which strategies to use and when, employ the Will-Skill-Thrill idea to identify which to use most often. If a strategy increases all three Will-Skill-Thrill in Students, then use it often; if it increases two, then use it sometimes, and so on.

We encourage you to incorporate three Battery Charging Strategies from this chapter into your weekly repertoire for several weeks in a row. This repetition allows Students to develop competence and confidence in using the strategies and also the creative, critical thinking capacity by engaging and connecting with content in different ways. Once they have mastered those strategies, consider adding in a few more, while still utilizing the original three, to increase their repertoire they take out the door.

#FULLYCHARGED
CHAPTER 5: BOOK STUDY/ TWITTER CHAT QUESTIONS

1. What is one strategy you use to explicitly teach creative, critical thinking?

2. How have Students' critical thinking skills changed over the last few decades?

3. How does explicit instruction and practice in critical thinking, influence one's competence, confidence, and cognitive capacity?

4. Which two Battery Charging Strategies would help your Students immediately?

5. Identify three ideas that resonate with you from this chapter.

Please visit effectiveteachingpd.com or mbsimplesolution.com to watch the #FULLYCHARGED Author Chat about this chapter and participate in our 21 Day Challenge.

CHAPTER 6
Blooming Parents

"At the end of the day, the most overwhelming key to a child's success is the positive involvement of parents."

—Jane D. Hull

✳ ✳ ✳ ✳ ✳

"Even the worst Parents want their children to turn out better than they did. Even the best Parents have absolutely no idea what to do sometimes."

—PJ Caposey

It was a guys' weekend, and I (PJ) had met up with my buddies at Danny's house for the night. Danny was among the last of our core group of friends to get married and the only one of us left without children. There was nothing odd about that fact, as many choose not to have kids, or wait until they are a bit older. Moreover, my friends are not the kind to get too personal over a subject like that.

Danny LOVED kids. When we had family get-togethers, he was the one always playing the role of the "fun uncle," tossing kids in the air, playing tag, and coloring. Eventually the conversation of the evening turned to someone telling a story about their kids, and then someone blurted out, "Danny, when are you going to have some kids?"

His reply was perfect, vulnerable, and honest: "I really, really want to have kids; I'm just terrified that I am going to suck as a Dad."

We were just 10 guys out enjoying a "guys" weekend; yet surprisingly, we espoused great humility, truth, and wisdom for the next several hours as we discussed our own experiences. We shared our worst moments of parenthood and celebrated some of the lessons learned from our own fathers, some of whom had already passed. Everyone was entirely transparent. Everyone was entirely real.

Out of this conversation, a few things became crystal clear in my understanding of parenting:

- *Even the worst Parents want their children to turn out better than they did.*
- *Even the best Parents have absolutely no idea what to do sometimes.*
- *Despite the countless parenting books and blogs, there simply is no perfect playbook to being an effective Parent.*
- *Every Parent wants school to be part of their child's ultimate success story.*
- *The most profound lessons are taught (and learned) at some of the most random times.*

This discussion energized me. Even those of us who were loving and caring Parents (some of us are even educators), who had spent thousands of hours caring for children, could not identify a formula, per se, for raising competent, confident, compassionate, and creative, critical thinkers. What worked for one child did not necessarily work for another. The parenting strategies we shared were a combination of love, luck, instinct, and repeating what our Parents did to us. There really was no systematic approach to the "job" that most of us considered the most important aspect of our lives.

As a group, we would probably be labeled "educated, well-resourced, and engaged" Parents who have the education, support, and resources to attend our children's events, have sit-down dinners often and help with homework. Even with the resources we have, we still struggle, question, and fail sometimes. What about Parents who don't have what we have? Their frustrations are probably more acute.

"Barry's mom loved him, but she failed to understand that love and protection didn't need to be sacrificed for rigor and high expectations."

—Rosa Isiah

I (Rosa) met Barry when he was a bright fifth-grade Student, struggling with self-control in the classroom. His teacher, Mr. Smith, was a compassionate and dedicated educator, determined to support Barry. Mr. Smith understood that Barry had incredible potential and would never give up on him. He also understood that Barry's distracting behavior was a way to avoid classwork and learning. He hoped that Barry's mother would be more supportive of his attempts to pull Barry back into classroom community, as he had isolated himself. Fifth grade was coming to an end, and they were both running out of teaching and learning time before Barry went off to middle school.

Barry's mom didn't care for male teachers, and she was candid about her feelings. She felt that Mr. Smith was too demanding of Barry and not understanding enough. Barry had been in the foster system as a young child, and she felt he needed nurturing and support, preferably from a female educator. She made excuses for Barry's behavior and dismissed the Teacher's requests for follow-through and support. Barry's mom had limited control at home, lacking the structure and accountability that every child needs. She loved him, but she failed to understand that love and protection didn't need to be sacrificed for rigor, boundaries, and high expectations.

Mr. Smith did everything he could to connect with Barry. He gave him opportunities to make up work and held him accountable for assignments. Absent for a quiz? No problem, Barry could make it up. Lacking supplies for a project? No problem, Mr. Smith provided all materials. Needed reteaching to understand a concept? No problem, Mr. Smith made himself available before school and eliminated every possible excuse for non-engagement. Barry realized that Mr. Smith made it more difficult to disengage than to do the work. He realized that Mr. Smith was persistent because he cared for him. He cared and he demonstrated his caring in a different way than his mother did.

Barry craved and appreciated the accountability and structure that his teacher provided in the classroom. He believed that Mr. Smith believed in HIM. Barry's grades improved and he embraced being a scholar in Mr. Smith's classroom. His mother noticed the difference in Barry's grades and behavior. She decided to reach out to Mr. Smith for help and recommendations. Mr. Smith connected her with the school counselor, who provided counseling and parenting supports for Barry's mom.

Mr. Smith realized that Barry's mom was doing the best she could with the resources and parenting skills she possessed. Barry needed structure and accountability at both home and school, so they read about, discussed, and collaborated to strengthen her skills in those areas. With his mom's desire to grow in her parenting capacity and Mr. Smith's support and persistence, Barry was able to get the structure, accountability, and care that he needed at home and at school to reach his potential.

"His capacity as her father had to increase, not decrease."

—Julie Adams

"Hey, Mrs. Adams, can I talk to you for a minute?"

It was a Friday afternoon in late September, and I (Julie) was walking across the parking lot to my car. I was exhausted after a long week teaching middle schoolers and taking care of my own family's needs. "Sure, Mr. Jones, what can I help you with?"

"As you probably know, my daughter really enjoys being in your class, and I'm so thankful for that because things have been pretty rough for her, or us, after losing her mother last year."

"Of course. She has mentioned some of the things that have changed this last year. I'm glad that she decided to run cross country; that's a healthy way for her to manage some of the stress she is probably feeling."

"Yes, she started running because her mom, my wife, was a runner. She even wears my wife's sweatband while running. The thing is Mrs. Adams, she needs a mom. I was hoping that you could help fill those shoes? I'm afraid that she has started cutting herself and binging and purging, and I am way out of my league here and need help. I need help with all things related to how to raise my teen daughter. I don't know how to help her make healthy choices or deal with her daily, emotional roller-coaster and just get her to talk to me a little bit. That was my wife's department; now I'm alone. I just can't do it."

How many times have you been asked as an educator to help fill a void in a child's life? That was not the first time I had been asked, nor will it probably be my last. We willingly help fill the gaps, but we sometimes do a disservice when we do this in place of the Parent/s.

Though I was more than willing to help provide her some of the support she needed, and I still do, I could not BE her mom. In truth, he needed help in how to provide support in some of the ways his wife had. Her death could not be his excuse to step aside. His capacity as her father had to increase, not decrease.

His earnest request reminded me of the Chinese proverb: "Give a man a fish and he eats for a day. Teach a man to fish and he eats for a lifetime."

Some Parents need to increase their capabilities, not only for the sake of their child, but also to increase their own competence, confidence, creative, critical thinking, and compassion.

They CAN do this and we can strengthen, care for, and encourage them in the process.

ROCKET SCIENCE RESEARCH

This chapter explores the research and strategies that Parents need to critically think about the decisions they make in designing a home environment that strengthens, cares for, and encourages the young brain. As previously mentioned, parenting is a skill. Not everyone grew up with physically and emotionally healthy Parents and even if they did, the role is even more complicated in today's society.

While the research was found in many places, the three books—*Nurtureshock: New Thinking About Children, Your Child's Growing Mind,* and *The Teenage Brain*—provided a significant base of our research. The experts recommend the following to Parents to critically think about the logistics of creating a home environment that prepares the young brain to be #FULLYCHARGED and ready to learn.

PARENTING STYLES

Parenting style can influence everything from how much a child weighs, to how much competence, confidence, creativity, compassion, and critical thinking capacity a child has. It's important to ensure a parenting style is supporting healthy growth and development because the way we interact with our children at home profoundly influences them for life.

In 1967, Dr. Diana Baumrind, published a study, "Child Care Practices Anteceding Three Patterns of Preschool Behavior," and identified three initial parenting styles (authoritarian, authoritative, permissive) and their effects on children; researchers have since expanded it into five types of parenting. There are pros and cons in nearly all of them. Knowledge of these five styles, help us clarify approaches that increase our children's Maslow and Bloom success.

Helicopter

This parenting style is defined as "a parent who is overly involved in the life of his or her child." This Parent believes the best thing for the child is to intervene and fix all their struggles; sometimes because it is easier, and sometimes because the child just does not have the ability to do so. This style has become more common as the academic, athletic, and overall pressure to succeed at young ages has increased. In some circumstances, children are developmentally asked to perform at unrealistic levels, so Parents may feel the need to "help" increase their Student's success.

• Pros:

Despite the negative perception of Helicopter Parenting, it can have positive benefits, such as kids feeling supported, heard, and protected. *Parenting to a Degree* author Laura Hamilton cites studies showing that children with Helicopter Parents were more likely to graduate from college than those raised by less-involved Parents.

• Cons:

Helicopter Parents are often considered anxious and/or domineering. They may fear their children will be emotionally or physically harmed by adults or their peers if they don't step in. They believe their kids do not yet have the skills to be successful; therefore, they intervene in nearly all situations. This can hamper a child's ability to problem-solve on his own.

Free Range

Otherwise referred to as Permissive Parenting, the book *Free-Range Kids: Giving Our Children the Freedom We Had Without Going Nuts With Worry*, offers insight into this style, defining it as lenient Parents who feel it's important for kids to engage in free play, explore their natural surroundings, and spend large amounts of time unsupervised in order to develop confidence and reliance.

• Pros:

The 2004 study, "A Potential Natural Treatment for ADHD," notes a correlation between Free Range Parents and children with lower rates of ADHD, as children are often encouraged to make their own choices without a lot of rules and play in natural environments. A 2009 study, "The Risk Is That There Is No Risk," from the *International Journal of Early Years Education*, identified Free Range raised children as more creative, less likely to bully (or be bullied), and more able to regulate their emotions.

• Cons:

The negatives to this style are increased risk of child injury, dental health problems, obesity, promiscuity, academic, and respect for authority issues, and legal ramifications from children being left home alone.

Authoritarian

Authoritarians are the strictest parenting model. Expectations are high, while rewards and displays of affection are minimal. Obedience is expected, and there is no tolerance for misbehavior.

• Pros:

Advocates of this style say that it leads to well-behaved kids who have a clear sense of right and wrong, are well-mannered, tend to avoid harmful situations, and have little confusion about what's expected of them.

• Cons:

Donna Volpitta, EdD, founder of The Center for Resilient Leadership and author of *The Resilience Formula: A Guide to Proactive, Not Reactive, Parenting*, states that while children raised by authoritarians grow up to be obedient, "They rank lower in happiness and self-esteem. They tend to have difficulty with social competence and independence." Authoritarians may have obedient kids who do their homework and chores with minimal fuss, but they sometimes mature into resentful, withdrawn, unhappy adults who limit contact with Parents as they grow older. They also tend to develop chronic lying skills.

Authoritative

Authoritative Parents establish structure and routines without neglecting healthy communication and love. They encourage children's voice and choice in the decision-making process, and they provide the support and modeling the child needs to meet expectations.

• Pros:
Dr. Volpitta shares, "Children with parents who have authoritative parenting styles show the greatest levels of happiness and success....they are more capable and confident and are able to regulate their behavior. They tend to be the most resilient." They tend to develop competent and confident adults who have strong decision-making skills.

• Cons:
This type of parenting seems be the perfect balance of hands-off versus hand-on and doesn't appear to present any cons to a child. It can be battery draining for the Parent though as it is considered the golden standard of parenting: modeling, supporting, teaching, loving, discussing, providing feedback, and making continual adjustments as the child matures.

Uninvolved

Dr. Volpitta identifies these Parents as those who "generally lack any emotional involvement in their children's lives. They place few demands on their children. They typically meet their children's basic physical needs, but beyond that, they are not a part of their lives." Sometimes, they do not even meet Maslow needs; there are no known pros, but a variety of cons associated with this form of battery draining neglect.

Sometimes Parents don't fit into just one category and they utilize several approaches; some situations may call for more Free Range, and others more Authoritative.

Neuropsychologist Bill Stixrud shares in his book, *The Self-Driven Child*, that Parents should consider acting more like a consultant than a manager, especially a micro-manager. A consultant provides guidance in choices, but doesn't force one. Providing a child more control over choices, according to Stixrud, such as whether or not to do homework, gives a child a sense of control, which is vital to self-esteem. However, a consultant will also explain the pros and cons of a choice and encourage the child to make the choice that will allow him to do what he wants to do later, such as play baseball or a video game. A Parent who understands it is not his responsibility to force the child to do the work, but help him to understand the pros and cons of doing it, decreases power struggles and instills intrinsic motivation.

When we encourage and support Parents to be reflective and make adjustments to help our Students thrive both in and outside of school, we help create an environment that increases capacity, not decreases it.

NO APP CAN REPLACE A LAP

Nothing can replace reading to your kids. There is no app that can replace a lap.

Vocabulary levels, comprehension, and language skills drastically influence a child's success. Dr. Stephen Burgess explains in "Shared Reading Correlates of Early Reading Skills," that shared reading experiences in the home are a low-cost solution that improves: vocabulary, phonological sensitivity, bonding, aptitude, attitude, speech, listening and language development, comprehension, and attention span. It also decreases anxiety and is an excellent component of a healthy bedtime routine.

Readers are leaders. Reading with children increases the likelihood they will develop an appreciation for reading also. According to statistics from Scholastic, "Strong correlations exist between parental actions and the frequency with which children read. For example, among children who are frequent readers, 57% of Parents set aside time each day for their child to read, compared to 16% of Parents of children who are infrequent readers."

If Parents could strengthen Students in just one way, consistently reading and chatting about both fiction and non-fiction in a relaxed atmosphere is a powerful way to do so.

SCREEN USE AND MENTAL HEALTH

A recent report from UNICEF, "Children in a Digital World," surveyed the online experiences of youth around the world. They found that today's adolescents are the "most connected" generation, with over 30 percent of Internet users worldwide being under 18.

Though technology can expand access to education and work opportunities, there are serious concerns exacerbated by the Internet, including increased risk of sexual abuse, exploitation, child pornography, and sex trafficking.

There are also increasing concerns about the link between Internet use and mental health problems like anxiety and depression.

Following are the 2017 statistics about youth mental health from the National Alliance on Mental Illness found at NAMI.org:
- 1 in 5 youth have, or will have, a mental health disorder, which includes anxiety and depression
- 37 percent of youth with a mental health disorder drop out of school

- 70 percent of incarcerated youth have a mental health disorder
- 8-10 years is the average time between the onset of youth mental health symptoms and intervention
- 90 percent of youth who died by suicide suffered from an underlying mental health disorder

Experts recommend increased Parent and Staff education in these issues and connecting with the child's pediatrician, school experts, mental health experts, and other families with children who suffer from mental health issues to increase a child's success in overcoming the problems. They also recommend "focusing more on what children are doing online and less on how long they are online," according to the "Children in a Digital World" report. An hour on social media or playing a violent video game can have more negative effects than an hour playing a reading comprehension and critical thinking game.

Social media and online bullying pose particular concerns for the young brain. According to the Centers for Disease Control and Prevention, "Suicide is the second leading cause of death for children between the ages of 10 and 14. Nationwide, the suicide rate more than doubled from 0.9 to 2.1 per 100,000 middle schoolers from 2007 to 2014."

Guess what else increased during those years? Smartphone and social media use among kids ages 10 to 14; the first smartphone was released in June 2007.

According to the American Academy of Pediatrics, bullying has a "clear relationship" with suicidal ideation and behavior among children, according to a review of 31 studies. Cyberbullying is particularly troublesome because it extends beyond the school day; kids often can't seem to get away from it if they're online.

Bullying has been a thing for centuries, but social media bullying did not exist until 2007 when social media was introduced. Again, the suicide rate among middle schoolers more than doubled during this time. Experts say there is a direct correlation here and not a mere coincidence, since social media use in particular is linked to increased mental health issues such as anxiety and depression.

How concerned are Parents about cyberbullying? Each year, the "C.S. Mott Children's Hospital's National Poll on Children's Health" surveys over 2,000 adults to identify health topics that are a "big problem" for children and teens. The Top 10 health concerns for children in 2017 were:
- Bullying/cyberbullying (61 percent)
- Not enough exercise (60 percent)
- Unhealthy eating (57 percent)
- Drug abuse (56 percent)
- Internet safety (55 percent)
- Child abuse and neglect (53 percent)
- Suicide (45 percent)

- Depression (44 percent)
- Teen pregnancy (43 percent)
- Stress (43 percent)

It is the top concern for many Parents, and it should be.

What are the effects of an "always connected" lifestyle, and how can we best manage it?

Internet and social media use are probably not going to disappear anytime soon, so it's important to teach healthy online habits, starting in the home. Common Sense Media is a great resource and provides many ideas to consider when establishing household guidelines; we have included some of them in the Battery Charging Strategies section. Following are the results of their study on Parent and Teen online device use and addiction in the home entitled, "Technology Addiction: Concern, Controversy and Finding Balance":

- 59 percent of Parents believe their Teen is addicted to their device; 50 percent of Teens agree.
- 78 percent of Teens check their device at least hourly.
- 72 percent of Teens feel the urge to immediately respond to online messages.
- +70 percent of Parents and Teens say they argue about device use almost daily.

Dr. Frances Jensen shares in *The Teenage Brain* how online addiction is a real problem and should not be taken lightly:

> *"The compulsive need to be digitally connected happens on two levels, behaviorally and biochemically. Every ring, ping, beep and burst of song from a device results in an 'Oh wow' moment in the brain. When the new message or post is opened, the discovery is like a digital gift; it releases a pleasurable rush of dopamine in the brain...Internet addiction has much in common with substance addiction" (211-212).*

Several studies, including the 2018 study, "Screen Addicted Teens are Unhappy," conclude that more screen time coincides with less happiness in the young brain:

> *"Researchers found that teens who spent a lot of time in front of screen devices—playing computer games, using more social media, texting and video chatting—were less happy than those who invested time in non-screen activities like sports, reading newspapers and magazines, and face-to-face social interaction. The happiest teens used digital media for less than an hour per day. But after a daily hour of screen time, unhappiness rises steadily, along with increasing screen time."*

So more screen time causes more anxiety and depression, which can trigger a desire to have even more screen time.

What do screen time experts do in their own homes?

Dr. Jenny Radesky is the lead author of the most recent revision of the guidelines on media and children from the American Academy of Pediatrics. She is also the mother of two young boys. She shares her household device guidelines based on recent research in the article, "What the Screen Time Experts Do with Their own Kids":

> *"We're not a tech-averse household.*
>
> *She and her husband both grew up watching 'tons of TV' and playing video games. 'We have a big flat-screen TV,' Radesky says. 'I have a smartphone.'*
>
> *In fact, she says, as a doctor she may be more prone to distraction than he is: 'My husband's really good. His stuff is always just on the kitchen counter and he hardly checks it unless it rings. But if I'm on call, I have my pager on. If something is an emergency that's how I can be found.'*
>
> *For the kids, since they started school, the rule is 'no media on weekdays.' They unplug at family dinner and an hour before bed. They have a family movie night on Fridays, which is an example of the principle Radesky touts in her research, of 'joint media engagement,' or simply sharing screen time.*
>
> *On weekends, they allow the kids cartoons, apps and games like Minecraft. But more than just limiting time, says Radesky, 'I try to help my older son be aware of the way he reacts to video games or how to interpret information we find online.' For example, she tries to explain how he is being manipulated by games that ask him to make purchases while playing."*

Online interaction is probably not going to end. It's important for Parents to know the research related to online addiction and mental health, and how to establish appropriate guidelines for healthy habits in the home. If a child's mental health takes a negative turn, online activity should be one of the first things to consider adjusting.

LANGUAGE MATTERS

The industry has been inundated, and rightfully so, with information based on Carol Dweck's work pertaining to fixed and growth mindsets and Angela Duckworth's concept of grit. The fixed mindset believes that you are born smart and there isn't anything that can be done to increase intelligence. The growth mindset believes that one can increase intelligence and success by building on innate capacity with hard work, a desire to learn more, perseverance, practice, and the knowledge and ability to utilize different strategies. Duckworth's concept of grit as an absolute essential life-skill has also influenced our thoughts in allowing Students the luxury of a struggle (and the resulting growth), especially when we cultivate the growth mindset. While many schools are working on these ideas at the Teacher-Student level, more can be done to share this research with Parents.

The direct connection between these concepts and parenting is not one that is often explored at the Parent level. Think about it: we often spend a full-day of professional development discussing growth-mindset with Staff, but we sometimes fail to share this new paradigm with our Parent partners.

The bottom line is that the language we use with youth matters. What and how we praise our Students for at home and school can hinder or increase their success.

Stanford's analysis of this idea started two decades ago with the release of Carol Dweck and Claudia Mueller's study "Praise for Intelligence Can Undermine Motivation and Performance" and continued to include over 150 more studies. Their conclusion was simple. Praising a child's intelligence led to the desire to hear more praise. Earning praise became the goal of every task, something that researchers say often diminishes Student success in the long run.

Once labeled genetically "smart," a Student has an image and label to uphold. This becomes far more important than learning, growth, or creativity. Smart equates to good grades. Get them at all costs. Praise follows grades. This is the unintended expectation Parents place on Students, and it's often caused by word choice. This leads to Students who are afraid to take risks and never want to fail because they may miss out on the praise in which they have been conditioned to yearn.

Researchers share instead of praising Students' intelligence, affirm their grit, perseverance, willingness to learn and their use of strategies. And for goodness' sake, let them struggle sometimes.

Instead of praising in this way, "You're so smart and successful in math/music/athletics, and such, because it's in your blood!"

Praise this way, "You're successful in math/music/athletics because you are willing to practice extra, ask for help, try new strategies, and learn from mistakes. Most importantly, you don't give up, not even when it gets tough!"

THE POWER OF SHARED RESPONSIBILITY AND ROUTINES

In the article, "This is Why Parents Should Establish Family Routines," author and parenting expert Alyson Schafer, shares research from several large studies that conclude the tremendous benefit in establishing routines and sharing responsibility for chores and tips for doing so:

> "According to a 2012 study, 'Chaotic Homes and Children's Disruptive Behavior,' there's a correlation between chaotic homes and behavioural problems in children. Researchers at the University of Louisville,

Columbia University, New York University, and Virginia Polytechic Institute also found that the more chaotic a family's life is, defined by disorganization, lack of routine, excessive noise, crowdedness, and an overly fast-pace, the more likely their kids will encounter a string of issues, including: smaller vocabularies, lower IQs, more stress, higher levels of aggression, poorer sleep patterns, less positive relationships with parents and siblings, and worse overall health.

Tips for setting up new routines

1. Start small and be consistent
I can't stress this point enough. Just pick one simple routine you want to work on and don't tackle any others until this one is going smoothly. A good starting point might be clearing your plate from the dinner table, scraping the leftovers into the compost, rinsing your plate in the sink and placing it in the dishwasher. Don't tackle your biggest issues first.

2. Take time for training
Don't assume your kids know how to do everything. Sometimes, they must be taught. Scraping a plate takes some dexterity. Knowing the best way to load a dishwasher takes experience. Help them practice and learn what is expected. Your mindset should be that of a patient teacher instead of cursing them for being sloppy and doing things wrong.

3. Invite children to participate in routine-setting
Children are more likely to be co-operative if they feel they had some say in the rules and routines they are expected to live by. Of course this is an age-dependent factor, but live by the rule that the more say they have, the more cooperation you'll likely get."

Similar to the efficiency and serenity in a routine-oriented classroom, the same can happen in a home. The young brain appreciates the consistency of certain routines and conserves battery charge when it knows the expectation, such as clearing the table when finished eating, and has been provided support in how to meet the expectation. This is also an example of a small accomplishment in a daily routine that grows problem-solving skills (There are dirty dishes all over the table, how can it be fixed?), competence, and confidence.

ELIMINATE MULTITASKING AND ESTABLISH BOUNDARIES

Dr. Frances Jensen writes in *The Teenage Brain* about the wonderful strengths of the young brain, such as rapid knowledge acquisition and high energy levels, but also the need for guidance in ALL areas:

"It is important to remember that even though their brains are learning at peak efficiency, much else is inefficient, including attention, self-discipline, task completion, and emotions. Try not to overwhelm the young brain with instructions. Although they look as though they can multitask, in truth they're not very good at it. Even just encouraging them to think about what they need to do and when they need to do it, will help increase blood flow to the areas of the brain involved in multitasking and slowly strengthen them. This goes for giving instructions and directions too. Write them down, in addition to providing them orally, and limit the instructions to one or two points, not four or five. You can also help them manage time and organize tasks by giving them calendars and suggesting they write down their daily schedules. By doing so on a regular basis, they train their own brains.

Perhaps most important of all, set limits-with everything. This is what their over-exuberant brains can't do for themselves...the more on top of this you are, the fewer the temptations for your adolescents, and the fewer the temptations, the more their brains will learn how to do without constant distractions" (80-81).

SLEEP AND START TIMES MATTER

Sleep deprivation is at an all time high in our society. The National Sleep Foundation recommends 9 to 13 hours of sleep for the young brain ranging in ages 5 through 25. How much sleep does the young brain average? About six. Sleep is one of the foundational Maslow needs. In short, the young brain cannot demonstrate competence, confidence, compassion, creativity, or critical thinking when it is fatigued. Period.

In the study, "Sleep Deprivation Makes the Young Brain Resemble the Elderly Brain," researchers conclude: "Accumulating evidence supports that youth sleep deprivation and advanced aging have similar effects: decreased cognition performance and impaired brain function in execution, including vigilance, attention, and auditory perception, working memory and decision-making."

Dr. Judy Willis (*Research-Based Strategies That Ignite Student Learning*), Dr. Frances Jensen (*The Teenage Brain*), Dr. John Medina (*Brain Rules*), Dr. Eric Jensen (*Teaching with the Brain in Mind*), and Dr. Jane Healy (*Your Child's Growing Mind*) also conclude that sleep deprivation results in physiological, emotional, and cognitive deficits that make Maslow and Bloom success nearly impossible.

Sleep deprivation negatively impacts physiological health by causing:
- Skin conditions: acne, psoriasis, and eczema
- Extreme hunger and craving for unhealthy foods
- Slower reaction and response times

- Increased athletic injuries
- Slower recovery and healing rates
- High blood pressure
- Sensitivity to illness and decreased immunity
- Increased cortisol and inflammation throughout body

Sleep deprivation negatively impacts emotional health by causing:
- Aggression
- Impatience
- Impulsivity
- Decreased self-esteem
- Inability to regulate emotions
- Increased anxiety and depression

Sleep deprivation negatively impacts cognitive health by causing:
- Impairment of learning capacity
- Inhibition of creativity
- Hampered neural pathway connectivity
- Decreased problem-solving
- Increased forgetfulness
- Lower retention

During adolescence, circadian rhythms, or wake and sleep cycles, often change. This change is linked to the delayed release of melatonin, which is the chemical that triggers sleepiness. Due to hormonal fluctuations, environmental factors, and rapid brain growth many adolescent brains release melatonin two to three hours later in the evening than adult brains, signaling fatigue later than they should, which leads to a "wired in the p.m. but tired in the a.m." situation.

Dr. Judith Owens and colleagues concluded in the study, "Self-Regulation, Sleep Duration, Sleepiness and Chronotypes in Adolescents," that it's not just the amount of sleep that the young brain gets that matters, but also when it sleeps. Students who tend to be night owls and fall asleep later, report feeling sleepier and having less ability to self-regulate cognitively and emotionally throughout the day, even if they received adequate sleep.

The research and analysis corporation RAND recently concluded in "Later School Start Times in the U.S.: An Economic Analysis" that delaying school start times to at least 8:30 a.m., would save our country billions of dollars in academic remediation and behavioral interventions. It would also save money because health issues such as obesity, mental illness, stress, and student-related car crashes would decrease.

One of the most important components of a Maslow and Bloom healthy home is for Parents to make healthy sleep habits a priority.

GOT GUT SMARTS?

Gut health has garnered a lot of attention in recent years. Experts have discovered that there are just as many neural connections in our gut as there are in our brain.

Sit on that idea for a minute.

Much of our immunity and cognitive capacity are determined by our gut health. Gut health is determined by the balance between good and bad bacteria levels, and researchers are finding that those levels are linked to other chemical reactions throughout our body that impacts our cognitive capacity.

Dr. Siri Carpenter shares in his American Psychological Association article, "That Gut Feeling":

> *"The human gut is an amazing piece of work. Often referred to as the 'second brain,' it is the only organ to boast its own independent nervous system, an intricate network of 100 million neurons embedded in the gut wall. So sophisticated is this neural network that the gut continues to function even when the primary neural conduit between it and the brain, the vagus nerve, is severed.*
>
> *Gut bacteria also produce hundreds of neurochemicals that the brain uses to regulate basic physiological processes as well as mental processes such as learning, memory and mood. For example, gut bacteria manufacture about 95 percent of the body's supply of serotonin, which influences both mood and gastrointestinal activity."*

Research shared in the article, "Can the Bacteria in Your Gut Explain Your Mood?" provides further connections:

> *"Given the extent to which bacteria are now understood to influence human physiology, it is hardly surprising that scientists have turned their attention to how bacteria might affect the brain. Micro-organisms in our gut secrete a profound number of chemicals, and researchers like Lyte have found that among those chemicals are the same substances used by our neurons to communicate and regulate mood, like dopamine, serotonin and gamma-aminobutyric acid (GABA). These, in turn, appear to play a function in intestinal disorders, which coincide with high levels of major depression and anxiety."*

Neuropsychologist Jennifer Wolkin, shares in her analysis, "Meet Your Second Brain: The Gut":

> *"Poor gut health has been implicated in neurological and neuropsychiatric disorders. Disturbances in gut health have been linked to multiple sclerosis, autistic spectrum disorders, and Parkinson's disease. This is potentially related to pro-inflammatory states elicited*

by gut dysbiosis-microbial imbalance on or inside the body. Additional connections between age-related gut changes and Alzheimer's disease have also been made.

Further, there is now research that is dubbing depression as an inflammatory disorder mediated by poor gut health. In fact, multiple animal studies have shown that manipulating the gut microbiota in some way can produce behaviors related to anxiety and depression. Our brain's health, is dependent on many lifestyle choices that mediate gut health; including most notably diet (i.e., reduction of excess sugar and refined carbohydrates) and pre and probiotic intake.

We are now faced with the possibility of both prevention and treatment of neurological/neuropsychiatric difficulties via proper gut health. On the flip side, stress-reduction and other psychological treatments can help prevent and treat gastrointestinal disorders. This discovery can potentially lead to reduced morbidity, impairment, and chronic dependency on health care resources.

The most empowering aspect to the gut-brain connection is the understanding that many of our daily lifestyle choices play a role in mediating our overall wellness. This whole-body approach to healthcare and wellness continues to show its value in our longevity, well-being, and quality of life: that both physical and mental health go hand-in-hand."

Though this area of research is fairly new, it is worthy enough for us to educate Parents in so they can consider this aspect, especially when children are struggling emotionally and/or academically. Many of the environmental choices we make influence inflammation and chemical levels in our body, and that impacts our battery charge.

SET GOALS AND DREAM BIGGER

In 1946, the Medical Research Council launched a large, longitudinal study called "The National Survey of Birth & Development Cohort" focused on "how the environment at home and at school during childhood, affected physical and mental development and educational attainment. During adulthood, the main aim was to investigate how childhood health and development and lifetime social circumstances influenced their adult health and function and how these change with age." This British study started with over 13,000 newborns and has since been narrowed to focus on over 5,000, throughout a 70-year span.

One of the most important factors identified in the study of children who were healthy and successful was the value their Parents placed on growing their children's abilities, setting goals (dreams), and helping them reach their dreams. In other words, Parent competence, confidence, and critical thinking impacts Student competence, confidence, and critical thinking. A Parent's ability to see a child's capacity for greatness and to see them as a success, even when they are failing, are vital.

Even more important than being able to see children as a success, even when struggling, is the ability to communicate the possibilities of success to the child. Goal setting is a valuable part of that process. The study indicates that this parental behavior can literally have an impact on the entire trajectory of a child's life.

AIM FOR PARENT ENGAGEMENT, NOT JUST PARENT INVOLVEMENT

Larry Ferlazzo, author and educator, wrote the following about family engagement: "We need to relate to families not as clients, but as partners in school and community improvement."

Many schools have Parent *involvement*, but lack Parent *engagement*. Of course, any type of involvement is valuable, but what's the difference between involving our Parents and engaging our Parents?

Parent Involvement means telling Parents what our needs are and having them fill in the gaps. An example of involvement would be having Parents volunteer to plan a Student event or chaperone a field trip.

Parent Engagement, on the other hand, means asking Parents what their needs are via surveys and open forum discussions, developing relationships with Parents, and establishing a process that creates learning opportunities to meet those needs. Examples of Parent engagement include developing workshops in areas of need: literacy, math standards, English learner language needs, positive communication, and so forth.

The power in family engagement is the focus on empowering Parents as learning partners. We empower by listening to their wants and needs. When we provide opportunities for Parents to learn and build their teaching and learning capacity, we foster Student academic achievement. Our entire community of learners benefits from these engaging experiences.

Following are just a few ways our schools can be a welcoming place to serve Parents' Bloom needs and increase engagement opportunities:
- Host community college courses.
- Create public hours for school computer labs.
- Offer workshops on hot topics in education.
- Provide daycare options (this can be offered through high school Career Education courses).
- Offer foreign language courses and English language support classes.
- Offer GED support.
- Offer access to technology and free WiFi.
- Establish a Parent Resource center with rotating classes, resources and support offerings.

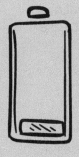

BATTERY CHARGING STRATEGIES
MEET PARENT BLOOM NEEDS & GROW THE 5Cs OF LEADERSHIP

Share the following strategies to get Parents #FULLYCHARGED with the knowledge and skills to establish a home environment that strengthens the young brain.

 ## LEVERAGE STUDENT EXPERTISE

A great way to teach and support our Parents is to leverage our Students' expertise. A family that learns together connects on a much deeper level and finds appreciation for the school serving their Students. Several examples and strategies provided would benefit from the incorporation of Student voice and modeling. A few quick examples include:

- Allow economics Students to provide the first part of a financial seminar for Parents.
- Have Students provide digital literacy/citizenship training for Parents.
- Have trained Students serve as conflict resolution specialists for their peers and train Parents on the same techniques they have been exposed to in their training.

 ## ESTABLISH A BEDTIME RITUAL

Following are natural melatonin-producing ideas Parents can incorporate into a healthy routine for Students, one hour before bedtime: turn off technology, take a warm bath or shower, brush and floss teeth, lower noise and bright lights, pick out clothes and pack backpack for next day, write down two or three things to be thankful for, take six deep breaths (five seconds in, five seconds out), get in bed and read from a hardcopy book (not a back-lit device), pray, or meditate.

 ## TAKE FIVE

There are a few five-minute chunks of time each day, in which positive Parent interaction can greatly influence a child's well-being: the five minutes after a child wakes up, the five minutes before the Parent and child separate for the school day, the five minutes the Parent and child first reunite after school, and the five minutes before bedtime. Having calm and positive conversations during these brief encounters helps to increase our battery charge.

CREATE A GUT HEALTHY ENVIRONMENT

To help good and bad bacteria levels in the gut be at an appropriate level, consider these ideas in your family's daily routine: drink half your body weight in ounces in water, eat fermented foods such as Greek yogurt and miso, reduce refined sugar, practice positive stress management such as exercising enough to break a sweat nearly every day, take a reliable pre/probiotic (consult a doctor for reputable choices), include organic fruits and vegetables, especially blueberries, bananas, garlic, and broccoli, avoid inflammatory items such as caffeine and dairy, and don't overuse antibiotics.

FOSTER A CRITICAL THINKING, TWO-WAY COMMUNICATION CULTURE

Set aside a few minutes each day to ask open-ended "low-stress" questions, be quiet, and listen to the answer. Try not to interrupt the child's answers. Compare and contrast and categorize things and ideas together. Instead of asking, "How was your day?" Ask: What are a few facts you learned today in your science class? How did the character in the novel you are reading fix a problem he encountered? Would you have solved it differently? What is the most popular thing to do at lunchtime, and why? If aliens came to your school and beamed up three interesting people to study, who should they take and why? How are your history classes from last year and this year similar and different? If you could teach the class tomorrow, what would you teach, and how would you teach it? What is one learning goal you have for each subject? What is one extracurricular goal you have for this year? How can I help you reach them? Perhaps one of the most important questions we can ask every day is: "How did you help and encourage someone else today?"

BULLY P.R.O.O.F. YOUR CHILD

Promote competence and confidence by meeting Maslow needs.

Role-play and discuss various responses before bullying happens.

Overtly practice gratitude, as bullied children sometimes forget all of the good things happening in their lives and focus more on the negative, making them seem bigger.

Open communication and regularly discuss online and social activity just as you do extracurricular and academic activity.

Forge an action plan if bullying happens, minimize or eliminate contact with the bully, notify adults and get help.

STOP-PRINT-BLOCK-TELL CYBERBULLYING

- Stop communicating with the bully; do not reciprocate the behavior.
- Print or screenshot the message as evidence.
- Establish a block so the person cannot contact you anymore.
- Tell a trusted adult and get help.

IS IT TRUE?

One strategy to employ when a child has experienced name-calling or bullying is to ask, "Is it true?" If a child has been teased for being a sore loser, then have a conversation about his actions when he loses to see if his behavior makes the name-calling true and then help the child make adjustments, if needed. If it is not true, then point that out also. Name-calling can be particularly harmful because a child will start to question whether the accusation is true. If it isn't, it helps to take the sting away.

MODEL COLLABORATIVE PROBLEM-SOLVING

Nancy Willard, the Director of Embrace Civility in the Digital Age, suggests Parents help children go through a series of mental exercises as a way to develop problem-solving skills. Help the young brain to set a goal of solving a problem, select a strategy to get there, evaluate that strategy for likelihood of success, and then, after trying it out, reassess the strategy for effectiveness. This collaborative problem-solving process helps the young brain think actions through and learn how to self-regulate, while increasing hope and clarity in how to increase success.

SET GOALS LIKE A SHARK

Shark Tank and business extraordinaire, Daymond John, shares this goal setting strategy in his book, *The Power of Broke*:

- Keep a running list of five to seven goals (health, relationship, family, learning, financial) on paper, add a completion date, and a few strategies to reach each goal.
- Use positive "I will" language to identify the strategies to be used to reach the goal: I will eat more fish, drink plenty of water and sweat for at least 30 minutes each day, to reach my goal weight by July 4th.
- Read through the list morning and night to stay focused and motivated. Add comments about progress.

ESTABLISH A HEALTHY MEDIA BALANCE

In the article "5 Simple Steps to a Healthy Family Media Diet," Common Sense Media explains:

> *"A healthy media diet balances activities (games, social media, TV), time (15 minutes? Three hours?), and choices (YouTube, Minecraft, Star Wars) with offline activities (sports, face-to-face conversations, daydreaming). At some point, kids will be able to manage their own media diets. In the meantime, these tips can help set them up for success. …*

> - Find balance. *Instead of counting daily screen-time minutes, aim for a balance throughout the week. Get your kids to help plan a week that includes stuff they have to do and stuff they like to do, such as schoolwork, activities, chores, reading, family time, and TV or gaming. Decide on limits and behavior using our Family Media Agreement.*
> - Walk the walk. *Put your devices away while driving, at mealtimes…, and during important conversations. Kids will learn habits from you.*

- Talk about it. *Ask questions about kids' favorite games, shows, and characters. Discuss ideas and issues they read about or learn about through a TV show or a game. This is an opportunity for bonding, learning, and sharing your values.*
- Create tech-free zones. *Set rules that fit your family, such as 'no devices during dinner,' 'no social media during homework,' or 'all screens off before bedtime.'*
- Check ratings. *Choose age-appropriate, high-quality media and tech for your kids."*

DIGITAL DETOX

Sometimes you just need to unplug for a little while. Consider one evening or 24-hour period each week, where all tech is turned off.

GROW THE GROWTH MINDSET

- Praise the controllable things: hard work, perseverance, problem-solving, positivity, and revision, instead of only intelligence.
- Personally apply growth mindset: have each family member share an area they struggle with and brainstorm how to improve in that area, then use the methods and share updates on improvements.
- Eliminate envy: instead of attacking another's success, identify the strategies that person used to attain success and how those can be applied personally.
- F.A.I.L.: discuss the acronym F.A.I.L. (First Attempt In Learning) and how it applies to learning a new skill; read about famous people and their failures, and share stories about personal past failures, what you learned and what you would do differently now.
- Focus on improvement, not perfection: when we focus on perfection, we often end up frustrated, so focus on growth instead.

FLIP PARENT NIGHTS AND SUPPORT

Educator Catlin Tucker (catlintucker.com), shares in her blog, "Flip Your Back-to School Night," how to utilize online resources to "flip" Parent Nights and increase outreach. She explains to Parents, via a QuickTime video posted online, how she uses tech tools such as Study Sync and Google Classroom with Students, and how Parents can find out what's happening in class, and access the web tools and resources to support their Students. Her strategies and tools can easily be expanded to provide online support to Parents throughout the school year.

FAMILY CODE NIGHT

Familycodenight.org is a national organization that provides FREE online coding introduction and games for K–5 Students and families. Schools host these nights for families and participants are immediately introduced to "Angry Birds" or "Plants vs. Zombies" characters and guided through how to progressively create simple code to manipulate the game elements. Have Students or an expert share some ideas regarding digital citizenship and safety as a great way to raise awareness about those issues also.

 # WHAT'S IN YOUR HEART?

Complete this activity with your child and compare ideas. When we focus on what we love, instead of what we dislike, our positive, critical thinking chemicals increase. Draw a heart and write or sketch inside of it the things you LOVE according to your five senses.

Consider these sentence starters to guide your thinking:

Two things I love to see are… Two things I love to smell are…

Complete for hear, touch, and feel too.

Next time you start focusing on the negative, remind each other about those wonderful things in your heart.

 # LIVE BY PRINCIPLE

It can be difficult to make good decisions when we are emotional. We can increase our success when we live by principles and commitments, instead of by feelings. For example, if someone is rude to you and you want to reciprocate, commit yourself to this Golden Rule principle: *Treat others the way you want to be treated.* When you are hungry and craving something unhealthy, commit to this principle: *You are what you eat so don't be fake, cheap, or easy.* When we live by our feelings, we often get drained. What are four principles you and your family can live by that will increase your emotional and/or physical health? Post them in a few places as positive reminders.

#FULLYCHARGED WRAP-UP

Parenting today is a tough gig. Our hyper-active, hyper-connected, hyper-social society makes it easy to lose focus on strengthening, encouraging, and caring for others. This must first start in our homes.

Parents at all points on the socio-economic spectrum are struggling with a variety of stressors, whether it's establishing boundaries, navigating screen time, or dealing with the loss of a spouse. We can help our Parents to "Bloom" by serving as a trusted resource for knowledge, strategies, and support so no Parent feels drained and all Parents feel #FULLYCHARGED and ready to raise up this next generation of leaders!

No "loving" Parent sets out to fail. Not a single one.

#FULLYCHARGED

CHAPTER 6: BOOK STUDY/ TWITTER CHAT QUESTIONS

1. What is one struggle that many Parents have today, that did not exist 20 years ago?

2. How does your school strengthen Parents in the Bloom realm?

3. What is one research topic from this chapter that surprised you?

4. Which two Battery Charging Strategies would help Parents immediately?

5. Identify three ideas that resonate with you from this chapter.

Please visit effectiveteachingpd.com or mbsimplesolution.com to watch the #FULLYCHARGED Author Chat about this chapter and participate in our 21 Day Challenge.

CHAPTER 7
Blooming Staff

"Those who know, do. Those who understand, teach."

—Aristotle

✳   ✳   ✳   ✳   ✳

"It had not occurred to Brandon that the new expectations he had for Staff were not being met because they lacked the skills necessary to meet them."

—PJ Caposey

One of the great privileges I (PJ) enjoy as a professional is the ability to coach and mentor new leaders. This endeavor, like most, is incredibly dependent upon relationships. It is my role as the coach to find a way to make it work, though there are some people that you just naturally click with better than others. I recently had the honor of supporting a new Principal, Brandon Zielinski, who is a younger, more energetic, skilled (and better) version of myself. We have many things in common and immediately developed a good rapport.

His school year started off as expected. Brandon immediately clicked with his Staff, and they discussed openly some of the struggles they had been encountering. Some items were easy; some were complex. But, he was delivering. Time and again, Staff would come to him throughout the first quarter, and he was able to fix or adjust things that had impeded progress in the past. This seemed like a match made in heaven.

As the year progressed, the onslaught of "fixable" items waned, and Brandon was able to get into classrooms more frequently, dig deeply into the school's data, and engage in meaningful conversations with Parents and other stakeholders. He was doing exactly what I would advise (he was both listening and learning), before attempting to lead.

Somewhere around mid-October, however, the progress seemed to falter. Brandon had discovered a handful of issues on his "listening and learning tour" and started to introduce ideas to fix these problems. For instance, Guided Reading was being implemented differently by almost every teacher, and strategy fidelity and benefit were lost. In other areas, the major focus of instruction was only on the content, not the skill development. And still in other areas, there seemed to be no implementation of the much-needed social-emotional learning curriculum.

Brandon went into "it's broken, let's fix it" mode. One week, he was introducing Project A, a week later Project B, and so on and so forth. By Thanksgiving break, the initial positive momentum was lost. He was no longer leading; he was fixing or attempting. Our conversations and coaching became even more meaningful at this point.

It had not occurred to Brandon that the new expectations he had for Staff were not being met because they lacked some of the skills necessary to meet them. When expectations are high but skills are low, stress fills the gap. Stressed learners, regardless of age, are not productive learners.

Brandon had to recalibrate and move from fixer back to relationship-builder, then to teacher, before he could reassume the role of leader. This was not an easy path, but it was a path worth traveling. Around April of his first year, Brandon had traversed the first major obstacle of his principalship. Teachers were learning how to implement the new strategies and curriculum with fidelity due to ongoing conversations, modeling, training, and support. Progress was being made. Relationships were strong, and the culture of the building was now a true professional learning community.

As the dust settled on the year, I asked Brandon for his reflections; they encapsulated what I have found to be true about meeting Staff Bloom needs.

He noted the following:
- *Adults, similar to children, do not learn under stress.*
- *If adults knew how to be great teachers, they most likely would be. If someone is not successful, the instructional leader must teach, support, and reflect with that person, not just direct him to improve.*
- *Change is complicated and you cannot force another human, let alone an adult, to change. You can only create the conditions for change (teach, support, reflect).*
- *Intentionally applying pressure to increase performance often drains batteries, as it increases stress. Improvement and learning do not typically exist in high-pressure situations.*

$$*\quad *\quad *\quad *\quad *$$

"The #1 requirement for a Teacher to be good, successful, and happy in the classroom...is not building relationships."

—Jennifer Hogan

A special thank you to educator Jennifer Hogan (thecompellededucator.com), for providing this thought-provoking narrative:

Just "being" a Teacher in the room can be easy. Keeping Students "comfortable," not confronting them with or coaching them to high standards, blaming Students for their failure...all of those things are easier than the really tough job of good teaching.

What does it take to be an effective Teacher?

The #1 requirement for a Teacher to be successful and happy in the classroom…is not building relationships.

Even before building relationships, a Teacher must have a positive "efficacy" mindset.

The Teacher must:

- *Believe in himself and his ability to build a positive relationship with Students and make a Maslow and Bloom difference.*
- *Love ALL kids.*

I once attended a wonderful PLC conference where I got to hear from Rick and Becky DuFour and others. I will always remember the four kinds of schools that Rick named and described:

- The Charles Darwin School: *"All Students can learn based on their ability."*
- The Pontius Pilate School: *"All Students can learn, if they take advantage of the opportunity we give to them."*
- The Chicago Cub Fan School: *"All Students can learn something, and Staff will help all Students experience academic growth in a warm, nurturing environment."*
- The Henry Higgins School: *"All Students can learn, and Staff will work to help all Students achieve high standards of learning."*

Henry Higgins was the professor in My Fair Lady *who turned Eliza Doolittle, a Cockney working-class girl, into someone who could pass for a cultured member of high society. At the PLC conference, Rick DuFour reminded us that Henry Higgins had more confidence, or sense of efficacy in his own abilities, than in Eliza. This was how he was able to successfully help her to rise to his expectations.*

Teachers with a "Henry Higgins" mentality believe that they can and will make a difference. Teachers must have confidence in their abilities to help Students meet their expectations. They must also have confidence in their abilities to adapt, build relationships, use the Maslow and Bloom tools in their toolbox, and lean on others when they need help.

This is not easy. This requires a positive and determined mindset.

Part of this mindset is having a love for both Students AND their success. Really analyze that idea. Don't gloss over it like a prospective Teacher in a job interview who wistfully says, "I want to be a teacher because I love kids."

- *Do you love the Students who dress in all black and wear fingerless gloves every day?*
- *Do you love the Students who don't sit down when you ask them to?*
- *Do you love the Students who roll their eyes when you tell them it's time to get to work on their assignment?*
- *Do you love the Students who have to be continually redirected?*
- *Do you love the Students who struggle academically and think they cannot be successful?*
- *Do you love the Students who don't say hello back to you, after you have smiled and said hello to them?*

Even before trying to build relationships, an effective Teacher loves ALL Students and wants them ALL to be successful.

Students are going to:
- *Check boundaries.*
- *Make sure that you mean what you say and your word is good.*
- *Find out if you can think on your feet.*
- *Ask you a question just to see what the answer will be.*
- *Analyze to make sure you're fair.*
- *See if they can find out what it takes for you to give up on them.*

We know this about Students.

When we love them, we accept that this is part of who they are. When we LOVE others, we make a commitment to them. We make a commitment to listen, forgive, care, accept, and, most important, do what it takes to help them succeed.

It takes this kind of mindset PRIOR to trying to build relationships. It takes a recognition of where Students are developmentally, accepting where they are on their journey, and doing everything we can to develop our own competence, confidence, compassion, and creative, critical thinking to help them be "Maslow and Bloom" successful.

THIS is what it takes to be effective.

THIS is what it takes to help them develop the same capacity.

*   *   *   *   *

"I can't imagine a better way to meet Staff Bloom needs than with the encouragement, development, and direct support of strong Teacher Leaders."

—Rosa Isiah

I (Rosa) have the pleasure of working with three Instructional Coaches. Instructional Coaches, or Teacher Leaders, have proven to be a transformational support for Staff and Students. Their support has led to deeper collaboration, improved instruction, and an increase in all Student learning as measured by benchmark, state assessment data, and school climate. I can't imagine a better way to meet Staff Bloom needs than with the encouragement, development, and direct support of strong Teacher Leaders.

Teacher Leaders have great strengths that benefit our school team; they are effective communicators, learners, and risk-takers who learn with Students, Staff, and Parents. Their support ranges from facilitating PD, to executing family nights, to leading Staff book studies. We meet regularly as a leadership team to analyze data, collaborate with individual Teachers and grade-level teams, and plan PD based on Student, Parent, and Staff needs. They meet Staff where they are and move and grow WITH them.

How do I know this?

I see it in the shy Teacher who is now opening her door and modeling lessons for Teachers from other schools.

I see it in the reluctant collaborator who now is eager to work with her grade level.

I see it in the retiring Teacher who is working closely with the Coaches, full of excitement and new strategies and energy for teaching.

Our Staff continues to grow and develop their teaching and learning skills as a result of the support from our instructional coaching team.

Rocket Science Research

Professional learning is a topic richly explored in educational research. This section will highlight what strengthens Staff to meet Student Bloom needs.

In order to best understand what works, keep these sentiments in mind:
- Applying pressure to increase achievement without training, support, and collaboration does not work.
- Drive-by, one-time trainings often do not impact achievement.
- Assuming an educator has the "will" to serve and strengthen our Students, poor instructional practice is more often a result of ignorance about the young brain and effective pedagogical methods, rather than defiance.

Does Teacher Leadership Capacity Influence Student Achievement?

In 2017, the Consortium for Policy Research in Education and the New Teacher Center published a study, "School Leadership Counts," that linked the development of Teacher leadership capacity to Student achievement.

Their key findings are as follows:
- Students perform better in schools with the highest levels of instructional and Teacher leadership.
- Specific elements of instructional leadership are strongly related to higher Student achievement:
  - ✓ Fostering a shared vision for the school
  - ✓ Providing an effective school improvement team
  - ✓ Holding teachers to high instructional standards
- When Staff are involved in decision-making processes related to school improvement planning and Student conduct policies, Students learn more.

Increasing leadership capacity in our Staff increases their competence and confidence, or efficacy, and it has a positive effect on Student achievement.

How Can We Strengthen, Encourage, and Care for Our Teacher Leaders?

Teacher Leaders play a monumental role in developing the 5 Cs in our Staff because their primary goal is to cultivate: competence, confidence, critical thinking, creativity, and compassion.

Teacher Leaders are great Teachers who have strong instructional skills and a thirst for improved instruction across the school site. They model lessons, co-teach, lead inquiry groups, and analyze data as part of their collaborative work with Staff. They support all by creating the conditions for effective instruction and learning at high levels. Teacher Leaders have to build trusting and honest relationships with team members before they can be seen as a resource in the classroom.

This process takes time, will, and skill, and it leads us to wonder:
- How do we develop Teacher Leaders?
- Who provides the leadership and instructional support?
- When do Teacher Leaders obtain their professional learning?

Rosa is an expert in growing Teacher Leadership. She shares these questions and strategies to support and grow Teacher Leaders who, in turn, grow our Staff:
- Meet Regularly: Work with your instructional leadership team regularly to plan, analyze data, and discuss their personal growth, gains, and needs. As a principal, Rosa feels a sense of urgency about instructional leadership and she learns just as much from her leadership team as they do from her.
- Build Professional Learning Community: Does your coaching team collaborate with job-alike peers across the district? This is a great way to enhance their expertise and coaching skills.
- Provide Time: Teacher Leaders need to build time into their day to process, research, and learn.
- Tap Into Resources:
  ✓ Human Resources: Rosa has been able to budget three part-time Instructional Aides into her school budget. They work closely with the Teacher Leaders to support Students with intervention and enrichment. Is this a possibility for your school?
  ✓ Fiscal Resources: What do the Teacher Leaders need to be most successful? Though we have limited budgets, materials, books, and conferences are a priority. Promote learning for all and invest in those opportunities that grow your Teacher Leaders.

Teacher Leaders help meet the Maslow and Bloom needs of an entire school community. They plan and deliver the best instruction and learning for Students, Parents, and Staff. As they engage in this great work, ensure that *they* are also growing and building capacity to increase collective efficacy.

TEACHER EFFICACY

As mentioned in Chapter 4, Staff competence and confidence (efficacy) impacts Student achievement. In *Visible Learning*, John Hattie describes Teacher efficacy as a Teacher's confidence in the ability to promote Student learning and overall Student achievement. Years of research indicate that the greater a Teacher's efficacy, the greater the impact on Student achievement. Hattie's research also indicates that collective efficacy, the shared belief by a group of Teachers that together they can positively impact and increase achievement, has the *strongest* positive influence (1.57 effect) on Student achievement and can yield over three years of Student growth in just one year. The impact is even more powerful than individual connections or home environment.

What improves Teacher efficacy?

- Making Mistakes and Taking Risks: It can be challenging for educators to take risks in their teaching and leading. Many equate mistakes with failure. Those who are open to making mistakes and taking risks, learn with their Students and create a culture where mistakes are a natural part of everyone's road to success.
- Positive School Culture: A healthy school culture has as much impact on Teacher efficacy as a toxic culture. Healthy school cultures nurture a growth mindset and risk taking, characteristics that build a Teacher's confidence in the ability to make a difference in the lives of Students, Parents, and other Staff. A toxic culture can strip away confidence and willingness to collaborate or seek support.
- Professional Learning Communities: Strong professional learning communities (PLCs) can have a tremendous impact on Student achievement and Teacher efficacy. The ability to collaborate effectively with others, share failures and successes, and analyze data to improve teaching practices builds *collective* efficacy.
- School Leaders: Administrative support greatly impacts a Teacher's belief in their own ability to teach ALL Students. School Principals can support efficacy by:
  - ✓ Creating opportunities to collaborate. Principals can provide release time for grade levels to collaborate, co-teach, or observe and learn from each other's teaching.
  - ✓ Building instructional capacity. Principals can provide Staff with opportunities to observe Staff at other sites and districts, work closely with a peer or instructional coach, and attend seminars or workshops.
  - ✓ Creating opportunities to provide Teacher-led professional development by highlighting their expertise and sharing their work also builds instructional capacity.
  - ✓ Including Teachers in shared decision-making. Teachers are experts and important stakeholders in a school community. Their voice is vital when making decisions that impact instruction, school culture and climate, and professional development.
  - ✓ Listening and providing genuine support and praise. Rosa shares that when she was a Teacher, the best administrator she ever worked with was an amazing listener and supporter. She was genuine in her praise and made Rosa feel like she was an important member of the team. She empowered her and trusted her. School administrators who acknowledge, love, and respect their team members, help develop Teacher efficacy in the process.

When Teacher efficacy is nurtured in a positive learning culture, the results have a powerful impact on Students, Parents, and Staff. When Teachers feel supported, trusted, and empowered, Student achievement increases. Period.

INSTRUCTION INFLUENCES ACHIEVEMENT

Teacher efficacy involves efficient instructional methods. Efficient instruction increases achievement. Instruction does not need to be outstanding (sadly enough), but it does need to be effective to increase achievement.

Mike Schmoker synthesizes volumes of research in his book *Results Now*:

> *"The evidence is indisputable. Mortimore and Sammons (1987) found that teaching had 6 to 10 times as much impact on achievement as all other factors combined. Robert Marzano (2003) points to numerous studies demonstrating that two teachers working with the same socioeconomic population can achieve starkly different results on the same test: in one class, 27 percent of students will pass, in another, 72 percent—a life changing difference. William Sanders, known for his 'value-added' studies, found that just three years of effective teaching accounts on average for an improvement of 35 to 50 percentile points. That's in only three years. And the effects are enduring (Sanders & Horn, 1994). Eric Hanushek has found that five years of instruction from an above-average teacher could eliminate the achievement gap on some state assessments (Haycock, 2005). Indeed it has, and in entire districts (Schmoker, 2001b). One recent study shows that the best teachers in a school have six times as much impact as the bottom third of teachers (Haycock & Huang, 2001). Researcher Allen Odden and his colleague conclude that 'improved instruction is the prime factor to produce student achievement gains' (Odden & Wallace, 2003)" (9-10).*

Instruction influences achievement; yet, methods can vary drastically and still be effective. We posit throughout this book that we have limited cognitive capacity, or battery charge. To increase capacity, we first must meet Maslow needs such as hunger, safety, unconditional acceptance, and positive relationships. Once those needs are met, then we can tackle the development of creative, critical thinking to increase achievement. Some Students drain battery charge just trying to figure out what to do to connect with and retain the volumes of information they are expected to turn into knowledge across all of the content areas.

Critical thinking can be developed through direct instruction, small-group collaboration, independent work, project-based learning, and/or design-thinking. There is no one magic teaching strategy that increases achievement in every child; there are several, and a blend is recommended. There are, however, several components to include in supporting Teacher efficacy and instructional success, and Teacher collaboration appears to be the foundation in developing a repertoire of critical thinking strategies that strengthen our Students.

WHAT WORKS?

Stanford University's Linda Darling-Hammond, writes in, "To Close the Achievement Gap, We Need to Close the Teaching Gap," that research conducted by the Organization for Economic Cooperation and Development (OECD) identifies the benefit of on-going Teacher collaboration, "higher-performing countries intentionally focus on creating Teacher collaboration that results in more skillful teaching and strong student achievement. U.S. researchers have also found that school achievement is much stronger where teachers work in collaborative teams that plan and learn together."

Teachers who collaborate (particularly important when there are both new and experienced Teachers) experience higher levels of success, especially when collaboration focuses on how to: identify strengths and weaknesses, set goals, utilize effective strategies and assessment methods, make adjustments to instruction based on Student data, and provide multiple opportunities for Student revision and improvement

Arthur E. Wise identifies the importance of this collaborative process in the *Ed Week* article "Teaching Teams":

> *"Professionals do not work alone; they work in teams. Professionals begin their preparation in the university, but do not arrive in the workplace ready to practice. They continue their preparation on the job.*
>
> *In medical, legal, and architectural settings, the services are provided by experienced and novice professionals working together to accomplish the goal—to heal the patient, win the lawsuit, plan the building. The team delivers the services. The experienced professionals are accountable to the client for those services and are responsible for the performance of the novices. The novices do much, often most, of the work, but do so under supervision. Experienced personnel create structure and are prepared to step in when necessary. The novices learn by doing, with feedback and correction by mentors."*

An important distinction to make is: just because one has the will or credential to teach, does not mean that person has the Bloom skills toolkit to do so. Collaboration is the foundation to increasing the likelihood that Staff develop the skills they need to help Students succeed.

BRAIN MATURATION RATES DIFFER

Have you ever given an assessment that some Students failed? Of course. For many reasons (age, temperament, maturity, genetics, environment), they just developmentally had not yet made dendritic and synaptic connections to the content.

According to Dr. Margaret Semrud-Clikeman in "Research in Brain Function and Learning":

> *"The brain begins to mature even before birth. Although it continues to mature throughout most of life, the brain does not mature at the same rate in each individual.*
>
> *This should not be surprising. After all, our bodies grow at different rates — we reach puberty at different ages and our emotional maturity at different times as well. Why should our brains be any different?*
>
> *Just because you have a classroom full of students who are about the same age doesn't mean they are equally ready to learn a particular topic, concept, skill, or idea. It is important for teachers and parents to understand that maturation of the brain influences learning readiness. For teachers, this is especially important when designing lessons and selecting which strategies to use."*

Should we then not give the assessment? No, go ahead and give it. But then allow those who were not able to demonstrate proficiency at that time to have more exposure and practice with the content to strengthen their understanding. Then, once the connections have been made, provide more opportunities for Students to demonstrate their increased proficiency.

How long will it take? Some Students just need a few more days, some weeks or months. The important idea here is to allow them the luxury of having that growth time and opportunity to increase and demonstrate their mastery.

BRAINS NEED BREAKS

Both young and mature brains need breaks because we have limited critical thinking capacity. Brain Breaks increase battery charge because they replenish neurotransmitters, which transport information throughout the brain. We share two types of Brain Breaks in the Battery Charging section, and we can incorporate them during Staff trainings and Student lessons to improve retention. Dr. Judy Willis explains the need for these in her book, *Research-Based Strategies to Ignite Student Learning*:

> *"Every brain needs periodic rests during which neurotransmitters can be replenished and executive function can process new material. The word 'Syn-naps' is an example of the use of word play to help build memory. The synapse is the gap between nerve endings where neurotransmitters like dopamine carry information across the space separating the axon extensions of one neuron, from the dendrite that leads to the next neuron pathway. The creation of a word like syn-naps helps teachers recall that after repeated release of neurotransmitters from a nerve ending, there needs to be a brain rest when the neurotransmitter can*

be restored to be available for release when the next message comes traveling along the neuronal circuit.

These syn-naps are restorative breaks that are as important for successful memory retention as are other elements such as surprise, positive emotional state, sensory memories, and other relational memories. Not only do these 'naps' prevent overloading of the circuits and interference with maximal memory storage conditions, they also maintain positive emotional states...it is ideal to prevent burnout by planning brain rests before students display the first signs of glazed expressions or distraction" (26).

Strengthening Staff Bloom skills, by increasing their neuroscience and pedagogical knowledge, greatly increases their efficacy and influence on Student achievement.

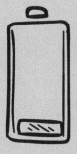

BATTERY CHARGING STRATEGIES
MEET STAFF BLOOM NEEDS AND GROW THE 5CS OF LEADERSHIP

Consider these strategies to get Staff #FULLYCHARGED with the Bloom SKILLS that cultivate pedagogical competence, confidence, compassion, and creative, critical thinking.

 ## TIME IS NEGOTIABLE; LEARNING IS NOT

Student success is the expectation, even if it takes longer than anticipated. Sometimes in school, the time it takes to learn is NOT optional, but learning IS. This mentality of "learn now or else" has sometimes led to a lot more "or else" and Student learning has been the sacrifice.

The entire purpose of teaching is to CAUSE learning. Therefore, whatever it takes and however long it takes, we must commit to the concept of learning as our goal. Some require more time and practice in order to make a dendritic and synaptic connection to our content, so it is helpful to teach Students a repertoire of creative, critical-thinking strategies and provide multiple opportunities for Students to practice them up and down Bloom's Taxonomy. Provide multiple ways for Students to demonstrate their proficiency, or to revise their deficient responses, as their levels of proficiency increase.

 ## NEURO NUGGETS

Yep, we've mentioned Neuro Nuggets a few times because they really do benefit Students, Parents, and Staff. The young brain is different, and it is HIGHLY influenced by environment. Some educators are not versed in neuroscience, so providing digestible "nuggets" greatly enhances our ability to meet Student needs. Provide short (30- to 60-second) Neuro Nugget ideas in morning announcements or longer segments in homeroom or advisory classes. Either way, everyone greatly benefits in learning about the young brain.

Consider choosing a theme for the week such as the benefits of sleep and sharing a little each day about the topic. Kidshealth.org is a great place to find doctor written articles about ALL things related to Student health.

Example Neuro Nugget:

> *"Did you know that neuroscientists recommend 9 to 13 hours of sleep each night for a young brain under 25 years of age? Sleep allows the brain to grow smarter because that is when it processes and connects to all that was experienced throughout the day. A sleep deprived brain often cannot think clearly, regulate emotions, control impulses or think as critically and creatively as a well-rested brain can. Do you get the recommended amount of sleep each night? If not, what changes can you make to catch more ZZZs? Thank you for thinking about this Neuro Nugget!"*

A few good books to serve as a resource include: *Brain Rules* (John Medina), *Research-Based Strategies to Ignite Student Learning* (Judy Willis), and *Teaching With the Brain in Mind* (Eric Jensen).

CHUNK LEARNING AND INCREASE STUDENT-CENTERED ENGAGEMENT

Create lessons that intentionally avoid the 20+ minutes of adult-dominated lecturing and instead vary materials, delivery, choices in tasks, assessments, seating, and learning products. "Chunk" lessons so the adult teaches and models for 5 to 10 minutes, then Students analyze, discuss, and practice the idea for 5 to 10 minutes, then repeat the short chunks throughout the class, especially during extended "block" periods. Set a timer if you're known to be a "sage on the stage," and stick to this model so at least half of class time is devoted to Student-centered learning and engagement.

RECIPROCAL TEACHING

Reciprocal Teaching is still considered an extremely effective comprehension strategy as it promotes metacognition, active reading, and collaboration. Place Students in groups of four, with each assigned a role: *summarizer, questioner, clarifier, predictor*. You can find sentence starters for each role online; provide them to Students at least the first few times this strategy is used. Have groups read a few paragraphs of an assigned text, using sticky notes and other annotation methods to monitor comprehension. After a few paragraphs, the *summarizer* identifies key ideas from the section, the *questioner* poses questions about confusing or important ideas, the *clarifier* attempts to clarify the confusing parts and make connections between the ideas, and the *predictor* makes predictions about what will be next in the text. Students can maintain their role throughout the lesson or switch roles for each section.

BLOOM SKILLS AND DEPTH OF KNOWLEDGE (DOK) TASKS

Bloom's Taxonomy is a classification of critical thinking levels, while DOK identifies tasks that can promote differing levels of critical thinking. Many educators now combine the two to assess levels of thinking.

To develop and assess Bloom's:

- "Remembering" and "Understanding" skills, utilize DOK Level 1 tasks: label, illustrate, calculate, recall, define, describe, identify who/what/when/why, and summarize.
- "Applying" skill, consider DOK Level 2 tasks: categorize, identify causal connections, interpret, predict, and sketch.
- "Analyzing" skill, use DOK Level 3 tasks: assess, cite evidence, draw conclusions, and hypothesize.
- "Evaluating" and "Creating" skills, incorporate DOK Level 4 tasks: compose, connect, defend, evaluate, design, and synthesize.

Keep in mind that each level of critical thinking can vary according to context. For example:

- *Describe* three characteristics of metamorphic rocks. (DOK 1: recall).
- *Describe* the difference between metamorphic and igneuos rocks. (DOK 2: determine differences).
- *Describe* a model you might use to represent the relationships that exist within the rock cycle. (DOK 3/4: understand the rock cycle and design ways to represent it).

 # THREE TRUTHS AND A LITTLE LIE

Similar to the popular game, this strategy can be a formative assessment during a lesson, or used as an exit ticket. Students write three facts (truths) learned from the lesson and then create a subtle false statement (lie) and quiz each other to check for understanding.

 # ANALYZE INFOGRAPHICS USING SCD

Educator Shaelynn Farnsworth (shaelynnfarnsworth.com) uses the SCD strategy to teach Students to analyze infographics:

> *"Structure: Infographics have a definite structure just as any other text students may read. The information presented is connected and not just a bunch of random thoughts put together. Have students determine how the information is organized.*

- *Is it Chronological? Cause and Effect, Inductive/Deductive?*
- *Is the information organized by person, event, product?*
- *Does the author use data or % to organize information?*

Identifying the structure of an infographic helps readers understand the flow of the information and is part of comprehending information.

Content: Infographics are constructed around content to help the reader understand complex ideas visually. Students should identify the story the visual content is telling the reader.

- *What is the main claim and evidence the author is using to support it?*
- *Where does the information come from?*
- *Is it reliable and current information?*

Only 53% of infographics contain data and numbers, have students key in on important words, phrases, and repetition. Most infographics chunk information into digestible, bite-sized segments. Identify the parts and how they relate to the whole.

Design: Infographics visually tell a story and relate information to consumers. Not only is content important in this form of communication but design elements help to convey meaning. Making students aware of design principles used in infographics is another strategy to support comprehension.

- *How is Typography used? Italics and bold-faced words jump out to the reader and signal important information.*
- *How are Colors used in the infographic? What information is emphasized through the use of specific colors? Do the colors relate to the content or topic?*
- *Spacing, alignment, and whitespace is used intentionally to focus the reader's visual cueing system, provide direction or flow, or connect like ideas.*
- *Finally, icons, numbers, images add to the overall understanding of the message, highlight important information, and help students visualize key points."*

 # QUESTION QUIZ GAME

Teach Students to form their own questions. Group Students by threes, provide them three to four minutes to write as many who/what/when/where/why/how questions as they can about a topic, with the minimum amount being at least six. They then prioritize the questions by importance, predict the answers for at least two of them, and then ask another group to predict answers for the same two.

#BOOKSNAPS

Educator Tara Martin (tarammartin.com) created #BookSnaps as a digital way for Students (and Staff) to annotate and share text. Use Snapchat, Instagram, SeeSaw, or Google Classroom to snap a picture of important text, whether it's to identify a claim and evidence or the rise, fall, and climax of a plot. Then annotate it, add a personal bitmoji and stickers, and post it to the social media class feed and on Twitter using the #BookSnaps hashtag.

DESIGN THINKING

Design thinking is the blend of art and science in the problem-solution process. Allow Students an opportunity to "Design Think" through at least one universal problem throughout a course. The process proceeds as follows:

- Define a problem.
- Brainstorm various solutions and choose the best.
- Create a model for your solution (use playdoh, write a paragraph, sketch an image).
- Test the solution, and share the results.
- Reflect and redesign it to improve the solution.

THE GRADUAL RELEASE OF RESPONSIBILITY

"One and done" does not work when teaching a new strategy such as "SCD," a Venn Diagram, or "Three Truths and a Little Lie." Students should have at least three opportunities to practice a method with support, before being held accountable for using it alone. Consider the following multi-step teaching process to increase Student success. Each time the strategy is practiced, the Students assume more responsibility:

- First, the teacher models it.
- Next, practice it with Students and provide descriptive feedback so adjustments can be made.
- Then, have Students practice it with a partner, and provide more descriptive feedback, if needed.
- Finally, have them practice the strategy individually.

BRAIN BREAKS

Young brains need breaks to reset their attention span clocks. Every 4 to 10 minutes, engage learners in a "Learning Brain Break" such as sharing with a partner three important facts just learned in the lesson. Every 10 to 20 minutes, incorporate an "Energizing Brain Break" to get learners up and moving around, even for just a minute or two, to reset their attention and increase oxygen-rich blood to the brain. Numb buns = lame brains!

 # THE STICKINESS FACTOR

The brain picks and chooses what it retains. Increase the likelihood of connection and retention with these five strategies from Dr. Eric Jensen:

- Provide repetition, retrieval opportunities, and review.
- Foster emotional and sensory connection (humor, visual, smell, tactile, etc.).
- Include quirky, unusual, and novel ideas.
- Reward learning with affirmation such as praise or a smile.
- Identify the WHY of a lesson, so Student buy-in increases.

 # VOCABULARY MASTERY

When introducing an important vocabulary term, it's often not enough to say it and define it. Consider a step-by-step process to teach the word and have Students write the information to study from to increase acquisition:

- Say the word, and provide the part of speech.
- Have Students repeat the word three to five times for fluency practice.
- Provide a Student-friendly definition.
- Share an example sentence using the word in context.
- Show a visual image to help make meaning "stick."

 # DIFFERENTIATE SUMMATIVE ASSESSMENTS

Multiple-choice responses, fill in the blanks, and short essay assessments are common. Following are seven differentiated methods Staff can use to assess Student proficiency:

- Ted Talks: Study a few Ted Talks, then have Students create and present one to demonstrate conceptual understanding; they are often a blend of narrative, fact, and a synthesis of both for the conclusion.
- Infomercial: Create a commercial about an important concept, and use persuasive techniques to "sell" the importance of that concept to an audience.

- Eulogy: Write a memorial speech for a fiction or nonfiction character with at least five to eight story references.
- News Report: Write a script summarizing the who, what, when, where, why, how details, and record their summary report "evening news" style.
- Singing Telegram: Create a song with at least two stanzas demonstrating concept proficiency, and perform it using Chatterpix.
- Scratch It: Create an animated review of a concept using scratch.mit.edu.
- Trivia Game: Create 10 to 15 review questions and answers to be used in a review game.

 # LEARNING LABS (CENTERS)

Centers are common in the primary grades, but not so much in secondary grades, though they can be extremely engaging and effective. One day each week, set up 10- to 15-minute stations for Students to rotate through that use different skills and mediums to learn content. One station might include watching a short video about the water cycle (or Boston Tea Party, etc.), and answering questions about it. At another station, Students are sketching a picture of the beginning, middle, and end ideas, and summarizing each sketch using specific content vocabulary. At a third station, they're reading an article about the topic and completing a 20-word News Flash synthesis, and a fourth station could have them working with a partner to complete a quick lab exercise, reenactment, or analysis of a pictorial about the topic. After completing the Learning Labs, have Students evaluate the type and level of their learning at each center, and synthesize the main ideas for closure.

 # HAND-RAISING ALTERNATIVES

If it's worth asking, then all Students should have the luxury and accountability of providing a response, not just the few who always raise their hands. Pose a question, allow at least 10 to 60 seconds of "think" time, then use one of these four methods to allow all Students to respond:

- Four Corners: If you think the answer is A, go to this corner, if it's B, go to that corner...
- White Board Responses: Students write their responses on personal white boards and share.
- Thumbs Up-Thumbs Down
- Structured Engagement: Students write their answer to a question using a sentence-starter provided by the Teacher, then share their answers in a "Timed Turn and Talk" with a partner (each partner has 10 seconds to share), then increase their speaking, listening, and accountability during Turn and Talk time by writing down one idea the partner shared.

VISUAL NOTE-TAKING

Sunni Brown's Ted Talk, "Doodlers, Unite!" is a worthy view. Visual note-taking such as sketchnoting, has gained popularity in recent years for good reason. Sketching images and linking them together allows information to be encoded in a new way and helps it to stick. Allowing Students to share and explain their images to one another also increases the retention.

 # ELIMINATE "I DON'T KNOW"

Critical thinking and creativity end when we allow Students to just say, "I don't know." Instead, have them respond with, "I don't know _____, but I do know _____." They can insert anything they know about the topic such as a vocabulary word and definition, a similar concept, or even make a prediction about the correct answer.

 # GRADES VS. FEEDBACK

The difference in how and what we communicate changes when we focus on why we communicate. Providing only a grade (versus a grade with descriptive feedback) serves different purposes. Putting a grade on an assignment and returning it so it is off of your to-do list and the Student "knows what he got" serves a different purpose than providing a grade along with descriptive feedback so Students know where they are and what they need to do to get to the next level of success.

Can you spot the difference in these examples? Which do you think would promote more Student growth and success?

8/10 - Good Job!

versus

8/10 - Great improvement, but the compound sentences still need work. Meet with me before or after school on Thursday so we can practice this skill. You are almost there!

 # BOOK STUDY: THE POWER OF POSITIVITY

Positivity increases battery charge because it increases the happy, critical thinking chemicals in our brains. Read Shawn Achor's *The Happiness Advantage*, and watch his popular Ted Talk, "The Happy Secret to Better Work" with Students and Staff, and implement the ideas into school culture. It is loaded with research, stories, and great strategies to maximize productivity; you will be positively thrilled that you did!

INCREASE EXPERTISE WITH DIGITAL PROMISE

Digitalpromise.org provides a series of micro-credentials to encourage and recognize Staff who continue to learn throughout their careers. They utilize networks, stories, research, and engagement opportunities in a variety of topics, to increase professional learning opportunities and efficacy in our profession. Expand your cognitive capacity and earn a micro-credential this week!

 # COLLEGIAL COACHING AND REFLECTION

Have Staff partner up to observe each other a few times per year. As they observe, they are not serving as experts, evaluating each other. They are simply collecting data in a certain area and helping a colleague to reflect. The observed teacher may ask a colleague to look for evidence that a certain strategy increases engagement and understanding or whether transitions are effective in minimizing distractions and maximizing instructional time. The observer collects the data, provides it to the observed teacher, and then asks reflective questions such as, "Why did you use that strategy at that point in the lesson?" "How do you remediate AND challenge Students at both ends of the skill spectrum during the lesson?" "Would you make any changes based on student achievement data?"

 # TWITTER

Twitter is a free and fun way for Staff to take charge of their own learning and connect with others outside their school walls. There are chats for every educational topic imaginable, book studies, hashtags to search for resources about a topic, and interactions with educators from around the world who love teaching as much as you do. Have a skilled Twitter user lead Staff through a tutorial and host various Twitter challenges each month such as: follow three new people this month and share an idea learned from each one at the next Staff meeting.

 # HAPPY "APPY" HOUR

Host an hour for Staff to learn, and play with one or two new apps or tech tools. Provide music and snacks to increase the fun.

#FULLYCHARGED WRAP-UP

Though it's popular to say, "Just build a positive relationship with Students," as Jennifer Hogan explained in her narrative, that alone doesn't make a Teacher effective or provide everything Students need to read, write, or critically think. Assuming Staff has the "will" to do what is best for Students, as PJ and Rosa wrote in their narratives, we must also provide training, support, and collaboration to develop collective efficacy, or in other words, competence, confidence, compassion, and creative, critical thinking skills, in both the Maslow and Bloom areas, in order to grow our Students' success.

#FULLYCHARGED
CHAPTER 7: BOOK STUDY/ TWITTER CHAT QUESTIONS

1. Would you categorize yourself as more of a Maslow or Bloom educator, or are you a skilled blend of both?

2. Think of a Teacher you know who has struggled in our profession; is it ignorance or defiance that has limited his/her success? How will you strengthen and encourage him/her?

3. How does your school cultivate Staff leadership?

4. Which two Battery Charging Strategies do you think would help your Staff immediately?

5. Identify three ideas that resonate with you from this chapter.

Please visit effectiveteachingpd.com or mbsimplesolution.com to watch the #FULLYCHARGED Author Chat about this chapter and participate in our 21 Day Challenge.

CHAPTER 8

Are You
#FULLYCHARGED?

"You cannot get through a single day without having an impact on the world around you. What you do makes a difference and you have to decide what kind of difference you want to make."

—Jane Goodall

"Because the only people who are crazy enough to think they can change the world are the only ones who ever do."

—Steve Jobs

We started Chapter 2 of this book with a quote from the late, great Dr. Rita Pierson:

> *"How powerful would our world be if we raised kids not afraid to take risks, who were not afraid to think, and who had a champion? Every child deserves a champion, an adult who will never give up on them, who understands the power of connection and insists they become the best they can possibly be. Is this job tough? You betcha. But it is NOT impossible. We can do this; we're educators. We're born to make a difference."*

To raise Students who take risks, we must develop their competence, confidence, and compassion by meeting Maslow needs and increasing social-emotional ecstasy. To raise Students who can think for themselves, we need to foster their creative and critical-thinking Bloom skills. And to strengthen adults who can champion these Students, we need to develop the same capacity in our Parents and Staff so they are #FULLYCHARGED and can serve in that role.

As she said, it's NOT impossible. We CAN do this.

What if we do ALL of this and our Students, Parents, and Staff do not become leaders?

A more pressing question is, what if we DON'T and they DO?

IT'S TIME WE HAD A TALK

Last year was probably the easiest year that you will have the rest of your professional life.

Yes, last year. Yes, last year when that new initiative was created by some committee, that you only half-heartedly adopted. Yes, last year when the "tough" class came rumbling and growling through your building. Yes, last year when you had more Maslow and Bloom struggling Students, Parents, and Staff than you could have fathomed. Yes, last year was the easiest year of the rest of your career.

You don't believe it?

Look around.

Ask your friends and colleagues. Find someone with 20 years of experience and ask if our role has gotten any easier. Ask if the demands, pressures, and sequence of changes are any easier today than they were in 1998 or 2008.

The answer is no. The answer is always no. The answer is no in our industry and in every other industry. We are in a constant race against time and progress, and they are not slowing down.

If you want to increase your efficacy and fulfillment, there are only two options:

- Option 1: Expect *less* of yourself. If you lower your personal expectations and settle for status quo, your professional life *may* get easier.
- Option 2: Expect *more* of yourself. In the famous words of Jim Rohn, "Don't wish for less problems, wish for more skills."

Get better. Serve. Strengthen. Persevere. Reflect. Grow. Then develop that same capacity in others.

The only way our profession charges you up is if your personal progress outpaces the progress of the problems.

Embrace struggle and change.

Appreciate when others bring their problems to you, because they see you as part of the solution.

Have a deep, hard, introspective conversation with yourself. Convince yourself that it is never going to get easier to make the profound impact on others that we are called to make. And be okay with that realization.

Don't settle.

You were not put on this Earth to be a drainer, or even a neutral status-quo.

You have chosen to be part of the most exciting and important profession in the world. We challenge you to BE the charger who creates the electrifying current of strength, care, and encouragement that lights up others along the way.

You have the chance to change lives every single day by increasing social-emotional ecstasy and skills in our Students, Parents, and Staff. Will you take it?

It is an awesome responsibility, but an even greater opportunity.

We hope, deep in your soul, that accepting that fact gets you #FULLYCHARGED!

APPENDIX A
Student Maslow Needs Assessment

Students can self-assess or educators can help with an assessment. If a Student does not respond with "Yes," provide an explanation so support can be provided.

1.   Do you receive adequate sleep and healthy food on a daily basis?

        Yes   Sometimes   No

Explain:

2.   Do you have appropriate clothing and shelter on a daily basis?

        Yes   Sometimes   No

Explain:

3.   Do you feel safe at home, and at school, on a daily basis?

        Yes   Sometimes   No

Explain:

4.   Do you have a positive and caring relationship, with at least one student, and one adult, at school?

        Yes   Sometimes   No

Explain:

5.   Do you have a positive and caring relationship with at least one person, outside of school?

        Yes   Sometimes   No

Explain:

6.   Do you feel that you are successful in at least one or two areas (chores, helping others, following rules), each week at home?

        Yes   Sometimes   No

Explain:

7.   Do you feel that you are successful in at least one or two areas (assignments, helping others, following rules), each week at school?

        Yes   Sometimes   No

Explain:

8.   Do you often feel you have the ability to learn new skills and be successful?

        Yes   Sometimes   No

Explain:

APPENDIX B
Adult Maslow Needs Assessment

Physiological

- Are you in healthy physical condition?
- Can you (physically) do everything you want to do?
- Have you made choices that promote a long and healthy life (regularly exercise, eat healthy, manage stress, limit screen time, etc.)?

Safety

- Are you financially secure?
- Do you feel financially prepared for retirement or a health emergency?
- Do you feel safe and secure at home, work, and in your community?

Love and Belonging

- Do you have engaging and meaningful personal relationships?
- Do you have positive relationships with your parents and kids?
- Do you have friends to connect with and feel emotionally connected to?

Esteem

- Do you respect yourself and feel respected by others?
- Do you find internal value in doing things for others, that do not result in prestige or financial gain?

Self-Actualization

- Do you have a strong grip on who you are and are capable of being?
- Have you become your best self?
- Are you a Battery Drainer or Charger?

APPENDIX C
The Myth of Colorblindness

The following article originally appeared on Rosa Isiah's blog (https://medium.com/@rosaperezisiah) on January 4, 2018.

> "It takes courage and practice to shift from a color
> BLIND to a color BRAVE ideology."
>
> —Rosa Isiah

Recently, I (Rosa) read a quote from a popular actor that troubled me. His words:

"The best way to stop racism today is to stop talking about it."

Interesting thought. Should we end poverty by not talking about it? Should we close the achievement gap by avoiding the topic? We could begin to change so much if we engaged in honest and courageous conversations about our biases, beliefs, and misconceptions. One of those misconceptions is the myth of *colorblindness*.

Colorblindness is the belief that we don't see color or race, that we see *people* and that we are all the same. These beliefs are widely held by wonderful and well-intentioned people, including educators. These are idealistic beliefs, but there are a number of issues with this ideology:

- We are beautifully diverse. Colorblindness negates our diversity, race, and culture.
- We all see color, and we all have biases. When we identify as colorblind, we are suppressing our authentic views and, in the process, perpetuating systemic racism.
- Race matters. It impacts opportunities, education, and income in many ways.
- Colorblindness oppresses people of color. When you fail to see color, you fail to acknowledge the current narrative, a system of injustice for many non-white people.

Why is the colorblind narrative popular?

For a few reasons. I believe it is easier to identify as colorblind than acknowledge differences that make us uncomfortable. This is easier for people to handle, especially in schools where we may lack the information and guidance to have difficult conversations about race. Another reason is simply not knowing; you don't know what you don't know. Many people also repeat what they've been taught and fail to reflect or question those beliefs. In the end, we don't realize how harmful the myth of colorblindness can be.

Why is this important in education?

When we work with children, we are responsible for their learning, social-emotional development, and overall well-being. We are charged with developing healthy relationships with our students and families. Part of this is embracing the gifts they bring to the classroom and using those diverse strengths to make learning more meaningful. This includes language, religion, culture, and race.

What can educators and ed leaders do to be color brave?

- Celebrate diversity! Acknowledge language, culture, and race as strengths.
- Build relationships with your students, and connect with families.
- Ask questions.
- Engage in honest conversations with your colleagues and administrators. Get comfortable with being uncomfortable and not having all the answers.
- Read and learn as much as you can about diversity and culturally responsive teaching. ASCD InService has useful resources: http://inservice.ascd.org/14-resources-on-culturally-responsive-teaching/ Another great resource can be found at Tolerance. org, Critical Practices for Anti-Bias Education: https://www.tolerance.org/magazine/publications/critical-practices-for-antibias-education/classroom-culture
- Provide culturally relevant student books. AmightyGirl.com has a great list of diverse books for children: https://www.amightygirl.com/blog?p=13481

It takes courage and practice to shift from a colorblind to a color BRAVE ideology. If we want to challenge racism and begin a wave of change in our country it must begin in schools with children and educators. Our students, all students, need you to lead this change. I hope this post inspires you to do so.

#FULLYCHARGED
REFERENCES

Achor, Shawn. *The Happiness Advantage: The Seven Principles That Fuel Success and Performance at Work*. Virgin, 2011.

Achor, Shawn. "The Happy Secret to Better Work." *TED: Ideas Worth Spreading*, May 2011, www.ted.com/talks/shawn_achor_the_happy_secret_to_better_work.

Adams, Julie. *Game Changers: 7 Instructional Practices That Catapult Student Achievement.* Healthy Learning, 2014.

Amen, Daniel G., and Tana Amen. *The Brain Warrior's Way: Ignite Your Energy and Focus, Attack Illness and Aging, Transform Pain into Purpose*. Berkley, 2017.

Armstrong, Patricia. "Bloom's Taxonomy." Vanderbilt University, cft.vanderbilt.edu/guides-sub-pages/blooms-taxonomy/.

Baron, Julie. "Three Things to Know about the Teenage Brain." *PsychCentral*, Aug. 2016, pro.psychcentral.com/three-things-to-know-about-the-teenage-brain/.

Baumrind, Diana. "Child Care Practices Anteceding Three Patterns of the Preschool Behavior." *Genetic Psychology Monographs*, 1967.

Blanchard, Keith. *Your Brain: The Art, Magic, and Science of What Makes You You*. It's All In Your Head, 2017.

Bronson, Po, and Ashley Merryman. *NurtureShock: New Thinking about Children*. Twelve-Grand Central Publishing, 2011.

Brown, Sunni. "Doodlers, Unite!" *TED: Ideas Worth Spreading*, Mar. 2011, www.ted.com/talks/sunni_brown.

"Bullying and Internet Safety Are Top Health Concerns for Parents." *National Poll on Children's Health*, 2017, mottpoll.org/reports-surveys/bullying-and-internet-safety-are-top-health-concerns-parents.

Bundy, Anita C., et al. "The Risk Is That There Is 'No Risk': A Simple, Innovative Intervention to Increase Children's Activity Levels." *International Journal of Early Years Education*, 28 Feb. 2009, eric.ed.gov/?id=EJ855900.

Burgess, Stephen. "Shared Reading Correlates of Early Reading Skills." *Reading Online*, 30 Nov. 2001, eric.ed.gov/?id=EJ669371.

Burke Harris, Nadine. "How Childhood Trauma Affects Health Across a Lifetime." *TEDMED Talk*, Sept. 2014, https://www.ted.com/talks/nadine_burke_harris_how_childhood_trauma_affects_health_across_a_lifetime

Butler, Heather. "Why Do Smart People Do Foolish Things? Intelligence Is Not the Same as Critical Thinking and the Difference Matters." *Scientific American*, Oct. 2017.

Caposey, PJ. *Making Evaluation Meaningful: Transforming the Conversation to Transform Schools*. Corwin, 2018.

Caposey, PJ, and Todd Whitaker. *Teach Smart: 11 Learner-Centered Strategies That Ensure Student Success*. Routledge, 2013.

Carpenter, Siri. "That Gut Feeling." *Monitor on Psychology*, American Psychological Association, Sept. 2012, www.apa.org/monitor/2012/09/gut-feeling.aspx.

Carter-Steward, Janice. *Motivating the 21st -Century Worker: A Case Study of Maslow's Hierarchy of Needs as It Applies to the Current Generationally Diverse Workforce*. 2009.

Centers for Disease Control and Prevention. *2012 National Survey of Children's Health*. National Center for Health Statistics, www.bing.com/cr?IG=27412417BFE74998A97640BDCC0F92DA&CID=18E9BBBE17D764BE022EB06E16786549&rd=1&h=mcgpCsURPZXw3mbnLBPmpW89amt2UQnQJGpqW-GptyY&v=1&r=https://ftp.cdc.gov/pub/Health_Statistics/NCHs/slaits/nsch_2011_2012/01_Frequently_asked_questions/NSCH_2011_2012_FAQs.pdf&p=DevEx,5066.1.

Chandler, Michael Alison. "Almost Half of D.C. Children Have Suffered a Traumatic Experience, According to Federal Survey." *The Washington Post*, 19 Oct. 2017, www.washingtonpost.com/local/social-issues/2017/10/19/f6e2f5da-b372-11e7-a908-a3470754bbb9_story.html?noredirect=on&utm_term=.0c432b6e0b7b&wpisrc=nl_sb_smartbrief.

Chapman, Gary D., and Paul E. White. *The 5 Languages of Appreciation in the Workplace: Empowering Organizations by Encouraging People*. Northfield Publishing, 2012.

"Confident, Relaxed and Happy Parents." *Parent Training*, www.parenttraining.com.au/resources/research/.

Darling-Hammond, Linda. "To Close the Achievement Gap, We Need to Close the Teaching Gap." *The Huffington Post*, 30 Aug. 2014, www.huffingtonpost.com/linda-darlinghammond/to-close-the-achievement_b_5542614.html.

"Deaths: Leading Causes for 2015." National Vital Statistics Reports, Vol. 66, No.5., National Center for Health Statistics, 27 Nov. 2017, www.cdc.gov/nchs/data/nvsr/nvsr66/nvsr66_05.pdf.

Donohoo, Jenni. "Fostering Collective Teacher Efficacy: Three Enabling Conditions." *Corwin Connect*, July 2016, corwin-connect.com/2016/07/fostering-collective-teacher-efficacy-three-enabling-conditions/.

Duckworth, Angela. *Grit: Why Passion and Resilience Are the Secrets to Success*. Vermilion, 2017.

Dweck, Carol S. *Mindset: The New Psychology of Success*. Ballantine Books, 2006.

Dweck, Carol, and Claudia Mueller. "Praise for Intelligence Can Undermine Motivation and Performance." *Journal of Personality and Social Psychology*, July 1998.

EdSource. "The Power of Parents: Research Underscores the Impact of Parent Involvement in Schools." 2014.

Farnsworth, Shaelynn. "How to Read Infographics: The SCD Strategy." 27 Dec. 2016, shaelynnfarnsworth.com/2016/12/27/how-to-read-infographics-the-scd-strategy/.

Ferlazzo, Larry. "Involvement or Engagement?" *Involvement or Engagement? Educational Leadership,* ASCD, May 2011, www.ascd.org/publications/educational-leadership/may11/vol68/num08/Involvement-or-Engagement¢.aspx.

Finley, Todd. "Are You at Risk for Secondary Traumatic Stress?" *Edutopia*, Oct. 2017, www.edutopia.org/article/are-you-risk-secondary-traumatic-stress.

Fisher, Douglas, and Nancy Frey. "Better Learning Through Structured Teaching: A Framework for the Gradual Release of Responsibility." *Learning, or Not Learning, in School*, ASCD, www.ascd.org/publications/books/113006/chapters/Learning,-or-Not-Learning,-in-School.aspx.

Frontline. "Inside the Teenage Brain." PBS, Jan. 2002.

"General Education Code 11504 Section Group." *Parental Involvement*, leginfo.legislature.ca.gov/faces/codes_displayText.xhtml?lawCode=EDC&division=1.&title=1.&part=7.&chapter=16.&article=.

Grossmann, I., et al. "A Route to Well-Being: Intelligence versus Wise Reasoning." *Journal of Experimental Psychology: General*, Aug. 2013, www.ncbi.nlm.nih.gov/pubmed/22866683.

Hafner, Marco, et al. "Starting School Later Would Boost the Economy." RAND Corporation, 30 Aug. 2017, www.rand.org/pubs/research_reports/RR2109.html.

Hamilton, Laura T. *Parenting to a Degree*. University of Chicago Press, 2016.

Hart, Betty, and Todd Risley. *The Early Catastrophe: The 30 Million Word Gap by Age 3*. American Educator, Summer 2003.

Harvard, Blake. "Less Is More: Simple Formative Assessment Strategies in the Classroom." *The Effortful Educator*, Dec. 2017, theeffortfuleducator.com/2017/12/10/less-is-more/.

Hattie, John. "The Applicability of Visible Learning to Higher Education." *Scholarship of Teaching and Learning in Psychology*, 2015.

Hattie, John. *Visible Learning: A Synthesis of over 800 Meta-Analyses Relating to Achievement*. Routledge, 2010.

Healy, Jane. *Your Child's Growing Mind: Brain Development and Learning From Birth to Adolescence*, 3rd Edition. Broadway Books, 2004.

Hogan, Jennifer. "The #1 Key for Being a Good Teacher." *The Compelled Educator,* Feb. 2018, www.thecompellededucator.com/2018/02/the-1-key-for-being-good-teacher.html.

Jensen, Eric. *Teaching with the Brain in Mind*. ASCD, 1998.

Jensen, Frances E. *The Teenage Brain: A Neuroscientist's Survival Guide to Raising Adolescents and Young Adults.* Harper Paperbacks, 2016.

John, Daymond, and Daniel Paisner. *The Power of Broke: How Empty Pockets, a Tight Budget, and a Hunger for Success Can Become Your Greatest Competitive Advantage.* Crown Business, 2017.

Kamenetz, Anya. "What the Screen Time Experts Do With Their Own Kids." NPR, 6 Feb. 2018, www.npr.org/sections/ed/2018/02/06/579555110/what-the-screen-time-experts-do-with-their-own-kids.

Klass, Perri. "Parents' Depression Linked to Problems in Children." *The New York Times*, 7 May 2012, well.blogs.nytimes.com/2012/05/07/parents-depression-linked-to-problems-in-children/.

Knorr, Caroline. "5 Simple Steps to a Healthy Family Media Diet." *Common Sense Media: Ratings, Reviews, and Advice*, 16 May 2017, www.commonsensemedia.org/blog/5-simple-steps-to-a-healthy-family-media-diet.

Krashen, Stephen D. *Principles and Practice in Second Language Acquisition.* Pergamon Press, 1982, www.sdkrashen.com/content/books/principles_and_practice.pdf.

Kuo, Frances E., and Andrea Faber Taylor. "A Potential Natural Treatment for Attention-Deficit/Hyperactivity Disorder: Evidence From a National Study." *American Journal of Public Health,* 1 Jan. 2004, experts.illinois.edu/en/publications/a-potential-natural-treatment-for-attention-deficithyperactivity-.

Lai, Emily. *Critical Thinking: A Literature Review*. Pearson Publishing, 2011, https://images.pearsonassessments.com/images/tmrs/CriticalThinkingReviewFINAL.pdf.

Martin, Tara. "#BookSnaps – Snapping for Learning." *R.E.A.L.,* Aug. 2016, www.tarammartin.com/booksnaps-snapping-for-learning/.

Martinez, Lorea. "Developing Teachers' Social and Emotional Skills." *Edutopia*, Nov. 2015, www.edutopia.org/blog/developing-teachers-social-emotional-skills-lorea-martinez.

Marzano, Robert. "Art and Science of Teaching/Relating to Students: It's What You Do That Counts." ASCD, Mar. 2011, www.ascd.org/publications/educational-leadership/mar11/vol68/num06/Relating-to-Students@-It's-What-You-Do-That-Counts.aspx.

Marzano, Robert J., et al. *Classroom Instruction that Works*. ASCD, 2001.

MAS Law Firm. "7 Ways Childhood Adversity Changes Your Brain." 15 Sept. 2015, dallasarealaw.com/7-ways-childhood-adversity-changes-your-brain/.

McBride, Karyl. "How Empathic Parenting Is the Antithesis of Narcissism." *Psychology Today,* www.psychologytoday.com/us/blog/the-legacy-distorted-love/201108/how-empathic-parenting-is-the-antithesis-narcissism.

Medina, John. *Brain Rules: 12 Principles for Surviving and Thriving at Work, Home and School*. Pear Press, 2014.

"Mental Health by the Numbers." NAMI: National Alliance on Mental Illness, 2017, www.nami.org/learn-more/mental-health-by-the-numbers.

"MetLife Survey of the American Teacher." MetLife, 2012, www.metlife.com/about/corporate-responsibility/metlife-foundation/reports-and-research/survey-american-teacher.html.

Morin, Amy. "4 Types of Parenting Styles and Their Effects on Kids." *Verywell Family,* Mar. 2018, www.verywellfamily.com/types-of-parenting-styles-1095045.

"National Sleep Foundation Recommends New Sleep Times." National Sleep Foundation, sleepfoundation.org/press-release/national-sleep-foundation-recommends-new-sleep-times/page/0/1.

"National Standards for Family-School Partnerships." National Parent Teacher Association, www.pta.org/home/run-your-pta/National-Standards-for-Family-School-Partnerships.

Owens, Judith A., et al. "Self-Regulation, Sleep Duration, Sleepiness, and Chronotype in Adolescents." *Pediatrics*, 3 Nov. 2016, pediatrics.aappublications.org/content/early/2016/11/01/peds.2016-1406..info.

Pierson, Rita. "Every Kid Needs a Champion." *TED Talks Education*, May 2013.

Race, Kristen. *Mindful Parenting: Simple and Powerful Solutions for Raising Creative, Engaged, Happy Kids in Today's Hectic World*. St. Martin's Griffin, 2014.

"Reciprocal Teaching | Classroom Strategy." *Reading Rockets*, 30 Oct. 2017, www.readingrockets.org/strategies/reciprocal_teaching.

Schafer, Alyson. "Why Parents Should Establish Family Routines." *HuffPost Canada*, 5 Jan. 2018, www.huffingtonpost.ca/2018/01/05/family-routines_a_23324919/.

Schmoker, Michael. *Results Now: How We Can Achieve Unprecedented Improvements in Teaching and Learning*. ASCD, 2006.

"School and Teacher Leaders Increase Student Achievement: Here's How." *New Teacher Center*, info.newteachercenter.org/school-leadership-report.

"Screen-Addicted Teens Are Unhappy." *ScienceDaily*, 22 Jan. 2018, www.*sciencedaily*.com/releases/2018/01/180122091249.htm.

Semrud-Clikeman, Margaret. "Research in Brain Function and Learning." American Psychological Association, www.apa.org/education/k12/brain-function.aspx.

Shapiro, Jordan. "Kids Don't Read Books Because Parents Don't Read Books." *Forbes*, 14 May 2014, www.*forbes*.com/sites/jordanshapiro/2014/05/13/kids-dont-read-books-because-parents-dont-read-books/#fe21abf25d50.

SJI Opening Doors. "Chris Blodgett: ACEs, Complex Trauma, and Resilience. SJI 2015 Annual Conference." *YouTube*, 8 Jan. 2016, www.youtube.com/watch?v=2boWzPsVBuI.

Skenazy, Lenore. *Free-Range Kids: Giving Our Children the Freedom We Had without Going Nuts with Worry*. Jossey-Bass, 2009.

Smith, Peter Andrey. "Can the Bacteria in Your Gut Explain Your Mood?" *The New York Times*, 23 June 2015, www.nytimes.com/2015/06/28/magazine/can-the-bacteria-in-your-gut-explain-your-mood.html.

Sternberg, Robert J. "The Nature of Creativity." *Creativity Research Journal*, June 2010.

Stevens, Jane Ellen. "The Adverse Childhood Experiences Study—The Largest, Most Important Public Health Study You Never Heard of—Began in an Obesity Clinic." *ACEs Too High*, Oct. 2002, acestoohigh.com/2012/10/03/the-adverse-childhood-experiences-study-the-largest-most-important-public-health-study-you-never-heard-of-began-in-an-obesity-clinic/.

Stixrud, William R., and Ned Johnson. *The Self-Driven Child: The Science and Sense of Giving Your Kids More Control over Their Lives*. Viking: Penguin Random House LLC, 2018.

"Stressed in America." *Monitor on Psychology*, Jan. 2011, www.apa.org/monitor/2011/01/stressed-america.aspx.

"Suicide and Suicide Attempts in Adolescence." American Academy of Pediatrics, Apr. 2018, pediatrics.aappublications.org/content/pediatrics/early/2016/06/24/peds.2016-1420.full.pdf.

"Technology Addiction: Concern, Controversy, and Finding Balance." *Common Sense Media: Ratings, Reviews, and Advice*, 3 May 2016, www.commonsensemedia.org/research/technology-addiction-concern-controversy-and-finding-balance.

"The Essential Supports for School Improvement." *UChicago Consortium on School Research*, The University of Chicago, Sept. 2006, consortium.uchicago.edu/publications/essential-supports-school-improvement.

"The State of the World's Children 2017: Children in a Digital World." UNICEF, 6 Dec. 2017, www.unicef.org/publications/index_101992.html.

"Title I, Part A: Parent and Family Engagement." California Department of Education, Mar. 2018, www.cde.ca.gov/sp/sw/t1/parentfamilyinvolve.asp.

Tucker, Catlin. "Flip Your Back-to-School Night." 15 Sept. 2015, catlintucker.com/2015/09/flip-your-back-to-school-night/.

Volpitta, Donna M., and Joel David Haber. *The Resilience Formula: A Guide to Proactive Not Reactive Parenting*. N.W. Widener Publishers, 2012.

Wadsworth, Michael, et al. "Cohort Profile: The 1946 National Birth Cohort (MRC National Survey of Health and Development)." *International Journal of Epidemiology*, 4 Oct. 2005, academic.oup.com/ije/article/35/1/49/849772.

Whitlock, Janis Leann. *Voice, Visibility, Place, and Power: Correlates of School and Community Connectedness among 8th, 10th, and 12th Grade Youth*. UMI, 2003.

Whitmire, Duncan. "Why Is Critical Thinking Difficult to Teach?" *Credo Education*, Apr. 2017, www.credoeducation.com/why-is-critical-thinking-difficult-to-teach/.

Willard, Nancy. *Cyber Savvy: Embracing Digital Safety and Civility*. Corwin, 2012.

Willingham, Daniel. "Critical Thinking: Why Is It so Hard to Teach?" *American Educator*, 2007, www.aft.org/sites/default/files/periodicals/Crit_Thinking.pdf.

Willis, Judy. *Research-Based Strategies to Ignite Student Learning: Insights from a Neurologist and Classroom Teacher*. ASCD, 2006.

Wise, Arthur E. "Teaching Teams." *Education Week*, Sep. 2004, www.edweek.org/ew/articles/2004/09/29/05wise.h24.html.

Wolkin, Jennifer. "Meet Your Second Brain: The Gut." *Mindful: Healthy Mind, Healthy Life*, 27 Aug. 2015, www.mindful.org/meet-your-second-brain-the-gut/.

World Health Organization. "Depression Fact Sheet 2017." 26 Mar. 2018, www.who.int/mediacentre/factsheets/fs369/en/.

Zhou, Xinqi, et al. "Sleep Deprivation Makes the Young Brain Resemble the Elderly Brain: A Large-Scale Brain Networks Study." *Brain Connectivity*, Feb. 2017, www.ncbi.nlm.nih.gov/pubmed/27733049.

ABOUT THE AUTHORS

Julie Adams

PJ Caposey

Rosa Isiah

Julie Adams (@adamsteaching) is a Nationally Board Certified Teacher, Educator of the Year, and a highly respected international consultant who has trained over 150,000 educators, coaches, business leaders, and parents since opening her firms in 2003. Her humor and expertise make her a popular Keynote speaker at leadership, athletic, and educational conferences across the country and around the world including: China, Indonesia, United Arab Emirates, South Korea, Hong Kong, Thailand, and Canada.

Julie taught for 14 years in kindergarten through graduate school and is the President and CEO of Adams Educational Consulting and MB Enterprise. She and her consulting team provide on-site training, parent and staff training videos, online training, coaching, and mentoring to teachers and administrators in both public and private schools. She also advises state departments of education and universities on educational policy, developmental appropriateness, and curriculum and instructional design.

She specializes in neuroscience, cognitive capacity, adolescent mental health, digital leadership, positive and systemic culture, social-emotional learning, instructional leadership, cognitive and instructional coaching, and best practices for literacy, critical thinking, and engagement.

She has been married since 1996 to fellow educator, Chris Adams, and they have two daughters.

Julie is also a best-selling author, providing practical strategies that increase student competence, confidence, comprehension, and success.

Her other books are:
- *Teaching Academic Vocabulary Effectively, Parts I–III*
- *PDP Cornell Notes: A Systematic Strategy to Aid Comprehension*
- *Game Changers: 7 Instructional Practices That Catapult Student Achievement*

Email Julie to speak at your next event at effectiveteaching@sbcglobal.net and check out her websites at: effectiveteachingpd.com and mbsimplesolution.com.

*   *   *   *   *

PJ Caposey, Ed.D. (@MCUSDSupe) is an educator and consultant, specializing in social media for leaders, educational leadership, school culture, teacher evaluation, student-centered learning, innovation, and the positive change process for individuals and organizations.

PJ is an award-winning practitioner, currently serving as Superintendent of Schools for Meridian CUSD 223 in Illinois, Adjunct Professor at Aurora University, Educational Consultant for MB Enterprise, and a Principal Coach for the Illinois Principals' Association. He is a highly sought-after speaker who has presented at the ASCD Annual Conference and the National Conference on Education, as well as many other conferences across the country.

PJ has been recognized as the Illinois ASA Superintendent of Distinction for the Northwest Region, IPA Principal of the Year, an ASCD Outstanding Young Educator Honoree, ASCD Emerging Leader, NSPRA 25 Superintendents to Watch Honoree, and a "40 Leaders Under 40" Honoree, among many others.

PJ has published three books, and his writing has been featured in a variety of different entities including: *EdWeek*, Edutopia, and the *Huffington Post*.

PJ is married with four children.

PJ's books include:
- *Teach Smart: 11 Learner-Centered Strategies to Ensure Student Success*
- *Building a Culture of Support: Strategies for School Leaders*
- *Making Evaluation Meaningful: Transforming the Conversation to Transform Schools*

Contact PJ to speak at your next event: pcaposey@mail.meridian223.org or via pjcaposey.com.

Rosa Isiah, Ed.D. (@RosaIsiah) serves students, parents, and staff as an elementary school Principal in southern California. Her experiences include 24 years in education as a Teacher, Bilingual Specialist, Language Arts Specialist, Assistant Principal, Coordinator of Federal and State Programs, and Principal. As Principal, Rosa focuses on supporting the development of a healthy school culture, professional learning communities, and meeting the needs of the whole child. She is passionate about equity in education and closing opportunity gaps for historically underserved students and believes in the power of relationships and leading with purpose and passion.

Rosa is a connected educator and the founder of #WeLeadEd Twitter chat. She is also the host of the WeLeadEd BAM radio show focused on Leadership through a Social Justice and Equity lens. Rosa was recently named 2016 Body and Mind Education Radio Thought Leader of the Year. She has contributed her voice to blogs, leadership books, and Education Week on the topics of leadership, school culture, English learners, and equity. In addition, Rosa is a Solution Tree associate and consultant for MB Enterprise, providing training in school culture, equity, and English learner success.

Rosa holds a BA in Sociology, an MA in Educational Leadership, a multiple-subject bilingual teaching credential, an administrative credential, and an Ed.D. in Educational Leadership for Social Justice.

She is married with two children.

Contact Rosa to speak at your next event: riisiah@gmail.com.